BRUNSWICK

The Story Of An American Company

The First 150 Years

Rick Kogan

Brunswick Corporation, One N. Field Court, Lake Forest, Illinois 60045-4811

Acknowledgements

My aim in this book was not only to trace the history of Brunswick Corporation but to convey it's flavor and tone at specific periods during it's 150 years. If I have been successful it has been with the help of many people. In this space, it would be impossible to thank them all: the dozens of former Brunswick executives, board members, employees, Bensinger family members and other observers who candidly shared the memories and graciously shared their momentos; the helpful staffs of the Chicago Public Library, the bygone Municipal Reference Library, library of the Chicago Historical Society, and the "morgues" of the *Chicago Tribune* and *Chicago Sun-Times*; Diana Haskell of the Newberry Library, Frances Forman of the Cincinnati Historical Society; Fannie Zelcer of the American Jewish Archives, and Ann Riker at the University of Illinois.; a vast number of writers and reporters whose previous words about Brunswick were of invaluable aid; any number of books that entertainingly and informatively chronicled the history of recreation and leisure in the country and throughout the world; the current employees, board members and executives of Brunswick who patiently gave their time and energy, especially Jack Reichert, whose honesty and thoughtfulness touch nearly every page; Dianne Yaconetti, whose fond feeling for and knowledge of the inner workings of the company proved essential to the understanding of Brunswick; and Gene Fisher, a born writer who masterfully steered this project and orchestrated many of the activities that attended the company's 150th anniversary. All of them have helped to shape this book. Without them I would have been lost.

Rick Kogan
March, 1995

About the Author

Chicago Journalist Rick Kogan has been a reporter, editor, critic and columnist for all of Chicago's major daily newspapers: the *Daily News, Sun Times* and *Tribune.* He has most recently served as the editor of the *Tribune's* daily *Tempo* section. He has been an on-air critic for WBBM-AM radio, on-air entertainment reporter for WBBM -TV and host of a weekly radio show on WLUP-FM called "The Sunday Papers." A native Chicagoan, he is author of the award-winning "*Yesterday's Chicago,*" in collaboration with his father Herman Kogan: "*Dr. Night Life's Chicago,*" a collection of newspaper columns; "*Sabers & Suites,*" a history of The Ambassador East Hotel; "*Teamwork,*" a history of the Wells Manufacturing Company and again in collaboration with his father, "*Pharmacist to the Nation ,*" a history of the Walgreen Company.

All correspondence and inquiries should be directed to Brunswick Corporation, One N. Field Court, Lake Forest, Illinois 60045.

Manufactured in Mexico by the R.R. Donnelley Company, Chicago, Illinois USA.

Design, production and photo research: Ligature, Inc. and Garfield-Linn & Company.

Dust cover illustrations by Yuri Kanzburg.

Contents

1 *Brunswick*

Through the years, the company started by John Brunswick has had many names. But to the public, it has always been Brunswick, a name that stands for quality.

There are but a handful of American businesses that date as far back into America's history as does Brunswick. Its story is one of risks and challenges—played out against a colorful backdrop of a century and a half of social, economic and technological change; the unpredictable nature of the economy, the public's capricious tastes, changing leadership and philosophies.

There are thousands of people who have played a part in this story—from the now-nameless workmen who helped John Brunswick make his first billiard tables in 1845, to Michael J. "Dad" Whalen, who invented the rubber bowling ball; from Ernest Hedenskoog, who worked for 40 years trying to build an automatic pinsetting machine, to E.C. Kiekhaefer, who transformed a broken-down outboard motor company into Mercury Marine, to the 22,000 employees around the world today.

There is no precise way to gauge the contributions of the company's many employees, past and present. One must inevitably look at the men in charge, for the company has mirrored their personalities, their characters and their visions.

For most of its existence, Brunswick was a family concern, owned throughout the 19th century almost entirely by the Brunswick and Bensinger families. In the 20th century, as the company's stock began to be dispersed into the hands of various descendants and to others through public offerings, the family relinquished its voting control. Nevertheless, for its key management, the company was led until 1966 by members of the Bensinger family. Remarkably, during Brunswick's 150 years, it has had only nine leaders.

When John Brunswick set out to make his first billiard table in a musty second-floor workshop in Cincinnati he had a seemingly simple goal: To make the best billiard table in the world.

Thus was born a corporate philosophy that continues to guide the company today. Brunswick's concerns for quality and craftsmanship formed an iron-firm foundation upon which all those who followed could build. And build they did.

Brunswick's son-in-law Moses Bensinger successfully moved the company into the bowling and bar furnishings areas. His son Benjamin's entrepreneurial spirit brought the company into such new and exciting areas as automobile tires, phonographs and records. In all those fields, only the best would do.

"My father was not happy making any except the finest quality goods," Benjamin Bensinger said of his father Moses.

Indeed, that philosophy propelled the company successfully through most of its first century and enabled Benjamin's son Bob to maneuver through the ravages of the Depression.

The nature of the company began to change dramatically in the 1950s, when the incredible success of the Automatic Pinsetter enabled Bob Bensinger's younger brother Ted to acquire 18 companies, including Mercury and Zebco. By so doing he started to transform the company into a conglomerate, into "the General Motors of Sports," as he was fond of saying. But with such intense growth came problems that eventually made necessary outside aide.

Jack L. Hanigan took over the Brunswick reins and helped cure its financial ills. He shared Ted Bensinger's conglomerate dream but his emphasis, and that of his successor, K. Brooks Abernathy, was not on recreation but on new technologies. They concentrated on the company's burgeoning medical and technical businesses and the home-grown defense division.

In 1982, Brunswick was rocked by a bitter takeover battle. To remain intact, the company was forced to dispose of its lucrative medical business. Under Jack Reichert, who took over at the time, the company, in his words, "began to focus on present businesses and try not to be something we are not."

In Reichert, who had once worked setting pins at a Wisconsin bowling alley, Ted Bensinger's "General Motors of Sports" dream again took full flight. Relying on values that had characterized Brunswick's long history, Reichert reemphasized the company's leisure businesses. He divested Brunswick of most of its non-recreational business and in 1986 made one of the boldest moves in company history by purchasing two of the largest boat building companies in the world, Bayliner and Sea Ray for nearly $1-billion.

The precarious, cyclical nature of recreational business would again rock the company in the late 1980s but after considerable and often painful streamlining, Brunswick emerged a stronger and more agile company, more firmly focused.

"Through the ups and downs, we have remained consistent," said Reichert. "We will strive for one thing: to be the best."

Those sentiments were echoed by Peter Larson, to whom Reichert passed what he called "the torch of leadership" in the spring of 1995 and who thus became only the tenth leader in the company's 150 years.

That is surely something John Brunswick would understand, a simple and sturdy philosophy—a star by which to guide a corporate ship into a successful future.

The Many Names of Brunswick

1845
John M. Brunswick

1858
J.M. Brunswick & Bro.

1866
J.M. Brunswick & Bros.

1871
J.M. Brunswick & Bro.

1872
J.M. Brunswick Billiard Mfg. Co.

1874
J.M. Brunswick & Balke Co.

1884
Brunswick Balke Collender Co.

1960
Brunswick Corp.

2 *Planting the Seeds*

John Brunswick comes to America where he builds his own small company into the world's largest billiard equipment firm

Before his 15th birthday, John Brunswick traded the peace and quiet of his hometown Bremgarten in the Rhine Valley to embark on an arduous and lengthy journey that would take him to an unknown future and certain adventure in the wilds of America.

The picturesque city of Bremgarten is a minor tourist attraction of Switzerland's Rhine valley. It is a place where change comes slowly, and guidebooks often point out its 11th Century bridge, which sits above the River Reuss near the center of town.

This is where a young mother died giving birth to her first child, John Moses Brunswick, on October 16, 1819. The child's father, Benedict, raised the dark-haired boy alone for two years, until he remarried and began another family.

Throughout his life, John Brunswick rarely talked about his childhood. His parents were Jewish and his nationality, since Bremgarten shared more characteristics with its northern neighbor than its own country, more German than Swiss. By all indications, his father was a kind man, but it is nevertheless likely that the boy felt increasingly like a stranger in his father's new family.

From travellers passing through town, he heard stories of America, compelling tales of a wild place across the Atlantic. It was not the land of opportunity that would inspire the immigrant waves of the late 1800s. Whatever stories young John Brunswick heard were not of

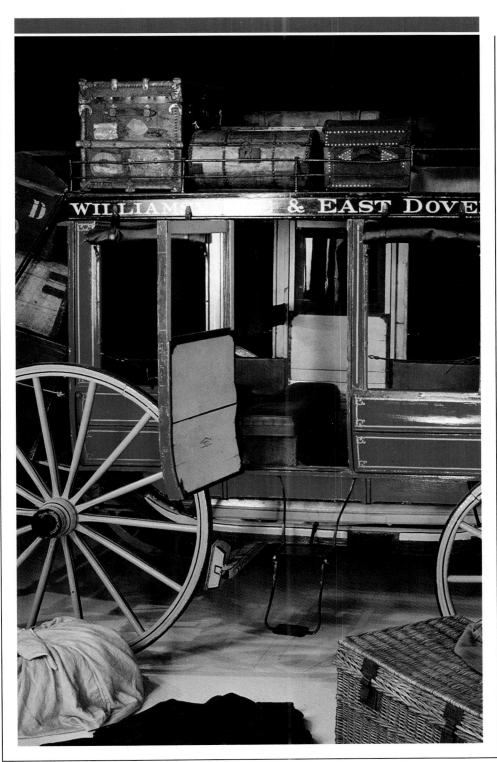

WILLIAM & EAST DOVE

Brunswick spent his first months in America dodging vehicles such as this one on the streets of New York. An observant young man, he determined that a prosperous future lay in the carriage-making industry and set about to fashion a career.

The sea voyage to America was long; and the discomfort, extreme. Grateful even to be alive, Brunswick huddled with other immigrants upon arrival in New York. Like them, he carried little more than some meager provisions and a few big dreams.

streets paved with gold but of a raw country of barely beaten paths.

It pulled him, though, away from the quiet of Bremgarten shortly before his fifteenth birthday, a sack of clothes across his back and a few coins in his pocket.

On foot he travelled to nearby Basel where he took a train, bounce after bone-jarring bounce, across Germany to the bustling North Sea port of Bremen. There he spent hours haggling over his fare. Shipping companies, which brought tobacco, cotton, and grain to Europe, had just begun returning to America freighted with emigrants. Sea captains and brokers shouted their deals from the pier, and some pressed crudely made

guidebooks into young Brunswick's hands.

The voyage by ship was long and the discomfort extreme. Brunswick was herded together with other emigrants and slept on a floor sparsely covered with sawdust. He carried his own meager provisions, for none were available on ship. He ate them cold, listening to the other passengers share their dreams and fears.

Some 40 days after setting sail, his ship arrived in New York's Manhattan harbor. There was no Statue of Liberty to greet Brunswick—she was more than 50 years away. On a warm late summer day in 1834, Brunswick stepped gingerly into America's largest city.

His first days in the city were confusing, but he was able to find work as an errand boy for a German butcher in the Wall Street area. The pace of the city was frantic, at once ominous and exhilarating. Day after day, Brunswick ran along the narrow and winding streets of the city, delivering packages to wooden cottage houses and brick buildings an amazing four or five stories high. He fought his way through packs of newspaper vendors, chimney sweeps, second-hand-clothes salesmen, itinerant repairmen, and strawberry vendors as they vied in shouting each other down. Gas lamps lit his darkness at the end of a day's work, and he returned to his rooming house exhausted.

Six months of that life was enough. How could he observe

life's possibilities amid Manhattan's frenzy? Carrying his belongings in a small bag, he took a train to Philadelphia. In less than a week, he found work with a carriage maker.

It was the job he wanted. In New York he had seen, and spent a good portion of each day dodging, the astonishing number of vehicles that raced along the streets. Among these were the clarence and rockaway, the landau and landaulet, the open coupe, the barouche, the phaeton for speed lovers, and the double tandem mail coach. The carriage-making industry was flourishing. In Philadelphia, it had begun humbly in a wheelwright's shop a few years before the Revolution. When Brunswick arrived, the local carriage-making business was prosperous and growing.

And how much better Philadelphia suited Brunswick. It was an austere place full of dark colors and rectangular avenues which were completely deserted after 10 o'clock at night. Charles Dickens commented, after walking the city's streets, that he would "give anything for a winding road."

Brunswick spent four quiet years in Philadelphia as an apprentice carriage maker, finally leaving for nearby Harrisburg and a position as journeyman with a German firm owned by a man named Greiner. Greiner's daughter, 17-year-old Louisa, spent an increasing amount of time at the

This view of Central Street shows the peaceful nature of Philadelphia during the four years Brunswick spent there learning to make carriages.

Running errands for a German butcher, Brunswick found New York's streets clogged with carriages of all shapes, sizes, and purposes, as was this stretch of Old Broadway in the 1830s.

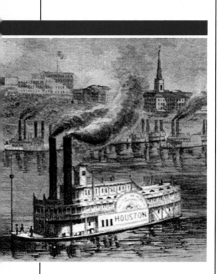

Coughing dark smoke into the valley air, steamboats line Cincinnati's docks— a vivid example of the city's prosperity in the 1830s.

shop, talking with Brunswick. Within seven months the two were married.

Brunswick moved into the Greiner house and continued to work for his father-in-law. His future seemed clear. When Greiner retired, his lucrative business would become Brunswick's. Clear perhaps, but too easy for Brunswick. He had not come to America to follow in another's footsteps.

In 1840 he and his wife moved to Cincinnati. Not only was it the most prosperous town in the west, it had a large German community in which the young couple would feel at home. During the 1830s, more than 30,000 Germans had moved to Cincinnati. The Miami Canal became their Rhine, and the place where the Germans lived was "Over the Rhine."

A writer at the time captured the scene: "One has no sooner entered the northern districts of the city lying beyond Court Street across the canal, than he finds himself in a foreign atmosphere— a foreign land. The people are Germans; their very gossip is German."

The city's principal industry was meat packing. So many stray pigs wandered the streets of the downtown area that the city was derisively but profitably called "Porkopolis." The waters of Deer Creek ran red with blood from slaughter-houses, and visitors marveled that carriages stopped to permit pigs to be herded across the street.

Some of those carriages were the handiwork of Brunswick, who was employed as a journeyman at a number of Cincinnati firms, including Bruce Brothers, Lawyer & Company, and Fulton Omnibus. When the latter company went out of business in 1841, as an unprecedented economic depression hit the country, Brunswick found himself out of work. Unable to latch on with another carriage-making company, he was finally forced to take a job as a steward on a river steamboat.

It was obvious to Brunswick that river commerce was immune to the depression. Along the Cincinnati riverfront, steamboats were often tied bow to stern for more than six miles, coughing thick black smoke into the fresh valley air. The system of inland canals branching out from the Ohio River had opened up the heartland, enabling farmers to move their products to the river for shipping to southern markets.

Steamboats stopped frequently along the Ohio and Mississippi to take on or put off freight. This river trading was commerce at its most fundamental, and it amazed such travellers as the poet Walt Whitman, who wrote:
"At one place . . . we shipped several hundred barrels of pork; ditto of lard; at another place, an uncounted lot of flour . . . besides

bags of coffee, rolls of leather, groceries, dry goods, hardware, all sorts of agricultural products, innumerable coops filled with live geese, turkeys, and fowls."

Brunswick could not resist. With what few extra dollars he could gather, he plunged into the trading. Though barely 22-years-old, he did well against older, more experienced traders. He was a tough haggler and surprisingly prescient in buy low/sell high commerce. He loved this new life, and he prospered. His health, however, could not withstand the rough-and-tumble river pace. Pneumonia forced him off the river and into bed for nearly five months. Once he recovered, his desire to return to the river was thwarted by his wife's pleas and his own fear of

Forced from the carriage-making trade by an economic depression, Brunswick took work as a steward on a riverboat that plied the Ohio River. He soon started trading goods and proved a natural. When he left the river, he had enough money to open his own woodworking shop.

Using crude tools such as the ones below, Brunswick and his employees worked long hours in his cramped and dusty shop making a wide variety of products—not only carriages, but cabinets and chairs, as well.

a relapse. He took the money accumulated from trading, rented a small workshop, and began his own carriage-making company on September 15, 1845.

The depression and competition in the carriage-making business was intense. Brunswick worked tirelessly, and hired only those men willing to match his long hours. He was demanding but fair, seeking the highest quality in the design and practicality of his products. Business went well. He moved to larger quarters and hired more woodsmiths. If there were no carriages to be built, Brunswick and his workmen made other items, including chairs, tables and cabinets.

"If it is wood, we can make it," Brunswick would tell his employ-ees. "And we can make it better than anyone else."

As his business increased, so did his reputation in the community. Socially, the self-made man was the hero of the day, embodying the highly respected qualities of courage, imagination, ingenuity, and self-confidence.

Brunswick became increasingly involved with local political, religious, and social groups. He was an active supporter of many Jewish organizations, spent many nights talking business at men's clubs, and began attending social events at the homes of other prominent businessmen.

At one such party, a lavish dinner gathering in 1845, the host took Brunswick aside and led him to a large room. In the middle stood a billiard table.

"This is a Thurston Superior," the host said proudly. "It's from England. Same fellow made a table for Napoleon. It's a fine table, isn't it? Feel the woodwork. . . . John, what do you think of it? Fine craftsmanship, no?"

Brunswick did not answer. He was transfixed, and for many minutes rubbed his hands along the finely carved wood of the table like a sculptor carefully examining a rival's work.

The first references to billiards in this country have little to do with the pastime. Tables were used for a variety of unsportsmanlike activities. They frequently functioned as everything from banquet tables and temporary morgues, to guest beds for up to six at a time, and operating tables. Paralleling billiards' earlier history in Europe, the game gradually found its way out of the homes of the upper classes and into taverns all along the colonial seaboard, where in a short time it became associated with drinking and gambling.

Puritans railed against the game. Still, George Washington played, and John Quincy Adams had a billiard table installed in the White House at his own expense, giving his congressional critics a chance to raise hell over his acquisition of "gambling furniture."

Though this image problem has dogged billiards to this day, there was another reason for the game's early limited popularity: crude playing equipment. It was a frustrating game, nearly impossible to master. Cue sticks were nothing more than tapered poles of ash or maple without leather tips. Table cushions were imperfect, consisting of cloth sleeves stuffed with

Early billiard equipment was crude and unreliable; nevertheless, this group gathered to do battle, and invite frustration, over a Virginia tavern billiard table in the early 1800s.

cotton, sawdust, feathers, or strips of felt. Table beds were made of warp-prone wood.

But in the decades preceding Brunswick's entry into the billiard business, a number of remarkable technical innovations began to transform the game.

● John Thurston, the most prominent billiard table manufacturer in England, had long searched for a proper cushion material. He experimented with horsehair, swanskin, Russian duck feathers, and even human hair. The results of those experiments were unimpressive, but Thurston found success in another facet of the game when, in 1826, he adopted a thick, warp-resistant slate bedding for his tables.

● A French infantry captain named Mingaud, jailed for unlawful political activity, whiled away his sentence playing billiards in prison. To soften the harshness of his stroke, and thereby cut down on miscues, Mingaud glued a piece of leather to the tip of his cue. He discovered that by striking the ball slightly off center, it could be made to do an astonishing number of things. He experimented for months, trying to understand his discovery. When his prison term expired, he demanded, and was granted, another month in jail so he could further investigate what became known as cue ball english.

● In 1835, the first crude rubber from India was substituted for cloth in table cushions. In the 1840s, it was discovered that by melting the rubber at different temperatures and mixing it with sulphur compounds, its elasticity could be increased and precisely controlled, its durability could be prolonged, and the problematic effects of temperature and humidity variations all but eliminated.

The advent of this better equipment and materials was a boon to Brunswick and other early billiard manufacturers, coinciding with America's emergence from non-athletic times. Until the 1840s, Americans had a distinct aversion to sports and exercise. The growth of popular sporting activities and events resulted from the growth of cities and the easing of living conditions. Before that time, it had been an academic question. It is hard to imagine a prairie settler, exhausted by daylong physical labor, enjoying sports in his leisure.

The range of sports in antebellum America was narrow. Baseball and football were not widely known before 1850. The principal spectator sports in cities were horse trotting, professional footraces, and competitive rowing. But billiards was coming on strong. Indeed, one of the major pre-Civil War sporting events was the first National Billiard Championship in Detroit in 1859, a match between Michael Phelan and John Seereiter.

Phelan's participation assured a big crowd. He was well known as a reputable manufacturer; two years before, he had patented a combination cushion that set new standards for tables. He was also an expert player, the author of two books on the game, owner of a billiard parlor in New York, and billiard columnist for several major newspapers.

Phelan and Seereiter met over four days in April, playing for an extravagant $15,000 purse. On the final night, more than 400 fans paid five dollars a head for seats in the gallery. Outside, another 4,000 people cheered as results were announced through a megaphone. Journalists from a dozen dailies filled the makeshift pressbox. Magazine illustrators scribbled on sketchpads.

Phelan and Seereiter, wearing vests and long-sleeved shirts, played brilliantly, each scoring as many as 50 points an inning. The lead seesawed back and forth. Just before dawn, Phelan stepped to the table leading 1,954 to 1,904. He ran the next 46 balls, winning the contest.

As this dramatic 1863 illustration shows, even the Civil War did not dampen billiards' growing popularity. This match, held in June in New York, attracted huge crowds. Michael Phelan was eliminated early, and the championship was eventually captured by Dudley Kavanaugh, here shown lining up a shot during the finals.

As John Brunswick and his craftsmen constructed their first billiard table, Brunswick had no hint of the game's potential. He was guided by an entrepreneurial spirit. Like the cabinets, tables, chairs, and carriages he was also making, the billiard table was another wooden item—an experiment in wood for which he hoped to create a market.

He did. His first billiard table customer, a successful local meat-packer, was so pleased with his purchase that he became a vociferous booster of Brunswick tables. One by one, other prominent citizens walked into Brunswick's workshop and ordered their own tables.

Within two years, orders for tables were arriving from cities as far away as Chicago and New Orleans. From the outset, Brunswick's tables were paragons of the woodworker's skill, eye-catching blends of function and form. Some of these early tables are outrageously ornate by today's standards, but the best of them, without stretching a point, can be called works of art.

For all of his appreciation for and understanding of aesthetics, however, it was Brunswick's business acumen that was primarily responsible for the company's early success. Sensing the need for expansion, Brunswick sent for his

This replica of one of Brunswick's earliest billiard tables speaks eloquently for its art and craftsmanship. Incorporating the latest technological advances, the table helped to popularize the game, quickly propelling Brunswick's company into leadership in the burgeoning industry.

half-brothers from Switzerland. As early as 1848, half-brothers David and Emanuel had established a sales office for him on State Street in Chicago. This branch quickly expanded to include a small factory and 8,000-square-foot billiard parlor on Washington Street, and a large factory on State Street. In 1852, a sales office was established in New Orleans, and in 1859 a salesroom and billiard hall were opened in St. Louis. Half-brothers Joseph and Hyman worked at the company's headquarters in Cincinnati.

All of the half-brothers played important roles in an aggressive business strategy. During the 1850s and 1860s, the Brunswicks engaged in vigorous competition with a number of smaller manufacturers. In addition, the company bought out suppliers of such raw materials as quarried slate and hardwood timber.

In 1858, the company was operating as J. M. Brunswick & Brother (half-brother Joseph). The following year, in a pamphlet called "Cincinnati in 1859," the company received the following profile: "J. M. Brunswick & Brother, salesroom and warehouse, No. 8 west Sixth street, manufacture annually, to the value of two hundred thousand dollars, of these tables. They work seventy-five

hands, and furnish equipment of every article in this line. Their tables are of the first quality and finish."

The company name changed slightly in 1866, to J. M. Brunswick & Brothers, when half-brother Emanuel was also listed as a principal. By 1869, when a song called "Billiards on the Brain" accurately captured the game's popularity, the fight for the biggest share of the billiard market was down to a three-company battle. Brunswick, along with son-in-law Moses Bensinger, who had recently joined the firm, vied with Julius Balke's Great Western Billiard Manufactory of Cincinnati for the burgeoning western market, and with Phelan & Collender of New York, which dominated the east.

A pair of ads (above) in an 1859 Cincinnati directory captures the rivalry between that city's two leading billiard manufacturers. It wasn't long, however, before Brunswick and Balke joined forces and started producing such lavish tables as the Monarch, trumpeted in such imposing ads as the one below.

3 *Back Bars and Bowling*

Brunswick's son-in-law, Moses Bensinger, propels the company into eventual dominance in the bowling and bar businesses

Lavish and detailed illustrations highlighted the Brunswick catalogue before the turn of the century as the company was selling almost as many billiard tables as it could make. And amid this prosperity the company's attention was grabbed by the potential of a sport called bowling.

Moses Bensinger had surprised many of his friends when he announced in 1867 that he would marry Eleanora Brunswick, the pleasant daughter of John and Louisa Brunswick. He further surprised those who knew him when he did not rush immediately to join his father-in-law's thriving billiard business, choosing to remain in Louisville and continue to work as an apprentice to a jewelry maker.

Bensinger's spirit of independence obviously appealed to John Brunswick. He talked occasionally with Moses about business, often after holiday celebrations at Brunswick's Cincinnati home. But it was not until 1869, shortly after Moses and Eleanora presented

him with a lively grandson they named Benjamin, that Brunswick employed his considerable sales skills to bring Moses into the family firm.

The battle with Balke and Phelan & Collender was intense and demanded more energy than Brunswick was able to muster. He had footsoldiers aplenty—the employees in his expanding company—but he lacked a trusted aide to lead his troops.

It will never be known what qualities Brunswick found lacking in his other three sons-in-law, but in Moses Bensinger he sensed some of his own ambition, intelligence, and business fortitude. Tragically, two of his own sons had died during the 1860s. Louis

Moses Bensinger, playfully posed with his wife Eleanora, would be proud to know that Brunswick bars made in the 1880s are still in use today. This striking model is the focal point of a popular Chicago restaurant.

Brunswick was a handsome 16-year-old when he drowned in the muddy waters of the Licking River, and Harry was barely 21 when he was trapped aboard a ferryboat as it burned after colliding with a barge on the Ohio River. His youngest child, Benedict Henry, born in 1860, was too young to become involved in business.

Brunswick relied increasingly on Moses Bensinger, who began as a salesman. In 1872, when the company was reorganized as the J. M. Brunswick Billiard Manufacturing Company, Bensinger was made a vice president, as were two long-time employees, A. F. Troescher and Leo Schmidt.

It was Bensinger who was the principal architect of the 1873 merger with Julius Balke's firm. The company name was changed to the J. M. Brunswick & Balke Company, and it was incorporated with a capital stock of $275,000.

During this period Brunswick was having considerable problems with his ambitious half-brothers. Especially troublesome appears to have been Emanuel, who started a rival billiard firm in Chicago. Pre-Chicago Fire records are virtually nonexistent, but a pamphlet published two years after the fire, in 1873, captures what seems to have been a heated battle between half-brothers:

"THE J.M. BRUNSWICK & BALKE COMPANY—Billiard-table Manufactory—62 Lake Street—was established in 1848, and is the oldest house in the Northwest; capital investment, $200,000; number of employees, 60; weekly payroll, $900; annual production, 700 tables, valued at $400,000. This company has furnished tables for Foley's Hall, the Matteson House, the Orient (St. James) Hotel, LaBerge's Hall, and many others. 350 of their tables have been put up, and are now in use in the city. Their trade extends from Canada to Mexico, and from the Alleghenies to the Pacific. Large rooms with their tables in every principal city in the West.

During an afternoon moment of relaxation, Moses Bensinger gets some liquid refreshment from Brunswick Vice-President A. F. Troescher.

"EMANUEL BRUNSWICK & CO.'s BILLIARD-TABLE MAN-UFACTORY—47 and 49 State Street—was established in 1853; capital investment, $100,000; number of employees, 65; weekly payroll, $1,200; annual production, 450 tables, valued at $175,000. Mr. Brunswick is the oldest manufacturer in this line in the West . . . Messrs. Emanuel Brunswick & Co. have the finest billiard hall on this continent, on Washington Street, opposite the courthouse."

What is one to make of this?

The pages of Chicago's city directories from the 1870's, though far from reliable or complete, present a dizzying number of Brunswick-operated businesses, at various locations. It makes for a strange puzzle, the solution to which has been buried by time. Whatever the nature of the relationships, Brunswick and his half-brothers eventually drifted apart. Emanuel, Joseph, and Hyman ran billiard parlors in such distant cities as San Francisco before eventually fading from the business. Solomon stayed in Cincinnati, where he devoted his time to writing light verse for local newspapers.

In 1879 Hugh W. Collender, following the death of his father-in-law, Michael Phelan, joined forces with Brunswick and Balke. When the company was renamed the Brunswick-Balke-Collender Company in 1884, the capital stock was increased to $1.5 million. Shareholders' meetings began to be

held regularly, and a board of directors was formed. Not only was the company the largest billiard equipment operation in the world, but it was larger than all competitors combined.

Moses Bensinger played a large role in the daily operations of the company, and as he concentrated on expanding the company to

The Brunswick catalogue was a feast of various products, among them some interesting and innovative variations on the game of billiards.

Though billiards was generally considered a man's game, one might still encounter a few accomplished woman players.

other cities, most notably Chicago, Brunswick remained in Cincinnati.

The strain of business was apparent. Looking at rare pictures of him, one sees an imposing figure with sharp features and piercing eyes. He wore a beard in the style of the times and it made him ap-pear as hard-edged and bone-tired as a Civil War general at the end of a bloody battle. But he continued to work long hours and became increasingly involved with local politics.

His interest had been kindled in 1870, when an admirer put his name into nomination on the Democratic ticket in his predominantly Republican ward. He lost that race by a surprisingly slender 48-vote margin. The next year, he was elected a Democratic state representative. He was an active legislator, introducing several important bills. One was an amendment to liquor laws whereby damages could be collected from "publicans, inn-keepers and others, for assumed injury to the relatives or friends of inebriates." This law was an early version of the current Dram Shop Act. Another of his bills called for prohibition of the practice of pharmacy by anyone who hadn't passed an examination.

Still, he was at his factory every day, and it was there, on the hot afternoon of July 23, 1886, Brunswick suffered a heart attack while examining some billiard tables about to be shipped to Chicago. He was carried back to his home on Grandview Avenue and put to bed. Two days later, he was dead.

Hugh W. Collender took over as president of the firm. He was the logical choice. But he was an old man and quickly the jockeying for position under him grew intense. For four years, Collender did little more than keep track of the company's balance sheets and accept the growing number of medals and awards it was winning at international exhibitions for the quality of its tables, racks, cue sticks, and balls. He barely noticed the infighting that surrounded him, most loudly the battle between Bensinger and Leo Schmidt.

When Collender died in 1890, Julius Balke bowed to his own age and ill health and all but gift-wrapped the presidency for the 51-year-old Bensinger. Schmidt was outraged and demanded out. Bensinger accommodated him, paying $300,000 for Schmidt's share of the firm.

Bensinger worked hard. And played hard, as noted in a frayed newsclipping: "An exciting race is scheduled to take place on the half-mile track at Crown Point, Indiana. It will be the old circus feat of man against horse, except that the race is to be modernized and the man mounted on a bicycle. Moses Bensinger will be the cyclist and the horse will be one of Will J. Davis' best trotters . . ."

Time has buried the race's outcome, but news of the event itself is a good example of Bensinger's character. This was a man who enjoyed challenges and risks. And was irresistibly drawn to products that would expand the company.

He reasoned that if tavern owners were in the market for a billiard table, they might also be interested in a bar. The company's woodworkers were designing elaborate billiard tables, and it followed that their creativity would find a natural extension in making bars.

Though the prospering billiard business allowed for few idle moments at the company's factories, Bensinger began to fill them with the design of bars. The workers responded, fashioning structures at once magical and imposing—stunning meldings of rich woods, flawless mirrors, and stained glass into elegant pieces of furniture.

Originally the bars were built on special order, but demand grew so great that the company was soon selling as many front and back bars as it could make. As waves of immigrants began their steady flow

Hugh W. Collender, who served as Brunswick's president from 1886 to 1890, was busy gathering awards that the company's products, such as the back bar below, were winning at international exhibitions.

into this country, urban populations swelled and with them the number of taverns. Many of these were plain, seedy places where a man might get a glass of beer for a nickel. Some taverns, seeking to elevate themselves from their shabby brethren, purchased a Brunswick bar. It was a sure sign of elegance and respectability—a touch of class.

Orders came from all major cities. The bars were produced at a factory in Dubuque, Iowa, whose location on the Mississippi allowed easy shipment to Canada and other markets. The orders that came from San Francisco had to make their way by ship around Cape Horn at the tip of South America.

The careful craftsmanship of Brunswick's woodworkers is evident in this finely detailed section of a back bar produced in 1891.

During the 1890s, newspapers were devoting space to the coverage of collegiate and professional sporting events. Little emphasis, however, was placed on participatory sports. The majority of Americans remained spectators.

Admittedly, there was a lot to see. Ice hockey was introduced to the U.S. in 1881, the year of the country's first lawn tennis match. Football scoring was standardized in 1884. Basketball was invented in 1891, golf tournaments began in 1894, professional football in 1895.

Most of these, however, with the exception of golf and tennis for the well-to-do, were not accessible or easily mastered by the proletariat. Bowling, on the other hand, was a middle-class delight. And Bensinger began to notice that many of the company's clients had installed bowling lanes in their taverns, and that those lanes were generally in use.

The popularity of bowling had grown steadily, if slowly, since it was first introduced to colonial America. An ancient game—a version of bowling is thought to have been played in Egypt as early as 5200 B.C.—it was first played on wide outdoor fields. Almost immediately it was set upon by Puritans, who believed it promoted gambling and laziness. The game, then called nine-pin bowls, or skittles, was banned in most of the 13 colonies. Eventually, some enterprising Connecticut settlers simply added a pin and argued with the authorities that the new game, ten-pin bowling, fell outside the prohibitory local ordinance.

The sport found its way indoors when restaurateurs and tavern owners realized they could attract customers by offering the amusement. They built lanes wherever they could, in basements or any sliver of space available. The first recorded indoor bowling match was played at the Knickerbocker Alleys in New York City on New Year's Day, 1840. At the time, there were some 200 bowling facilities in New York alone, prompting one British visitor to note that "of all species of [participant] sports, bowling was the national one in America."

Over the next decades, however, the number of lanes was far outstripped by demand, and the quality of surfaces and equipment was sorry at best. To remedy these matters, a group of 27 men, representing nine bowling clubs in New York, met in 1875. After lengthy discussions in the Germania Hall in the Bowery, three of the day's finest players were authorized to revise the rules of the

sport, draft new laws, and submit their actions to a larger committee called the National Bowling Association.

This organization was short-lived, but it managed to enact a few important rules: The center of the head pin was to measure 60 feet from the bowler's end of the alley, or the foul line; fallen pins were to be removed from the alley; and all balls rolled in the gutter were declared dead.

Jake Schaefer was one of billiards' early stars. Here he shows one reason why he was nicknamed "The Wizard."

In the cities, bowling proved an increasingly popular form of recreation. Here is a rare photograph of one of the first and best dressed women's leagues in New York City.

These rules were not universally accepted. Into the 1890s, the sport remained badly disorganized. The length of homemade lanes, the size of the balls and pins, and score-keeping methods varied widely.

But in this seeming chaos, Bensinger saw great potential. By the time he took over as president of Brunswick in 1890, he had already begun to oversee the company's first steps into the bowling business. As orders for pins, lanes, and wooden balls increased, he refined and enlarged Brunswick's capabilities to make them, carefully and quietly building a dominant company for a field in which domination was not yet warranted. He wanted to be at the starting line long before anyone else realized there was a race.

His influence had already been profoundly felt on the pastime of billiards. An accomplished player, he was frustrated by the fact that in three-carom billiards (otherwise known as straight-rail billiards), a good player could gather the three balls into one corner of the table and keep them there almost indefinitely while scoring.

The invention of the balkline—a thin chalk line drawn diagonally across each corner—and an early rule that allowed only one or two points to be scored consecutively within each triangular area helped little. Such stars as Jake "The Wizard" Schaefer spent the 1880s boasting that they had devised a method by which they could nurse balls gently against the rail, keep them close together, and score without missing as long as they desired.

Something had to be done, Moses realized, as he watched audiences doze during matches. He refined and perfected the balkline game, making it a challenge for the best players.

Equally interested in three-cushion and pocket billiards, his innovations there were of a technical rather than regulatory nature. He was constantly experimenting and researching, seeking better ways to make tables and equipment. A number of important patents for rubber cushions were registered in his name.

At best an average bowler, Moses had an even greater impact on that sport. He became bowling's biggest booster, bombarding the nation's leading bowling proprietors with letters. His argument was persuasive. The growth of the sport was stunted by its lack of standardized rules and equipment; if the sport were to grow it needed organization.

It took Bensinger five years to gather a group of bowlers and proprietors in New York City's Beethoven Hall. It was to be an informal get-together to discuss bowling rules and regulations. But by midnight of September 9, 1895, after hours of debate and eloquent speeches by Bensinger, the group had organized the American Bowling Congress.

He didn't stop there. He became the principal lobbyist for a national championship. And he got it in 1901, when the first ABC tournament was held in Chicago. Forty-one teams competed in the five-man event. The prize money was a substantial $1,200. Not coincidentally, all of the equipment used during that match, and for all ABC tourneys over the next 40 years, was manufactured by Brunswick.

Until Moses Bensinger convinced bowlers and proprietors of the need for a national bowling championship, most contests were impromptu affairs such as this 1892 battle.

4   20th Century Unlimited

Optimistic about the company's future, Moses Bensinger's son, Benjamin, prepares for further expansion and growth

More than a decade after the Chicago Fire of 1871 devastated the city, young B.E. Bensinger, Sr., began his career with Brunswick, sweeping floors in the company's factory.

In Cincinnati today, there are few vestiges of the Brunswick name. In the dusty files of the city's libraries and historical societies, one is lucky to find more than the briefest mention of the man or the company he built.

John Brunswick rode Cincinnati's boom years for all they were worth. But it was a later boom, in a bigger boom town, that eventually drew the company away from the banks of the Ohio to the shores of Lake Michigan.

Brunswick noticed Chicago's potential in the late 1840s, and over the next decades the city played an increasingly important role in the operations of the company. As the 1860s closed with a rush, Chicago was rich, the dominant city in the West. Its population was almost 300,000, nearly triple that at the beginning of the decade. The business district spread south and west from the river—79 bustling blocks of stores, hotels, and wholesale houses.

Potter Palmer, grown rich in merchandising and Civil War cotton speculation, owned three-fourths of a mile along State Street and was converting it to a street of merchants. There he built his Palmer House hotel and a "marble palace" that he leased to merchants Marshall Field and Levi Leiter. And there, two blocks south of the river and a block

By the 1880s, Brunswick was one of Chicago's most successful businesses, operating from this five-story building on State Street, at left, just down the block from the famous, and fire-proof, Palmer House Hotel, above.

St. Ignatius College Prep was one of the few buildings to escape the Chicago Fire. It still stands today and houses this magnificent library built by Brunswick craftsmen in 1872.

north of Field's store, stood an imposing five-story building, with a huge sign on top: "J. M. Brunswick & Bros."

Even the events of Sunday evening, October 8, 1871, did little to set the company back. Only three days after the Chicago Fire finally burned itself out—with a property loss of $200 million, 250 dead, and 20,000 homes and 17,450 other buildings destroyed—the city was bouncing back. And so was Brunswick, open for business with new goods shipped from Cincinnati.

Only 20 years after the fire, the city was bigger than ever. By 1890, its population of 1,208,676 placed it second only to New York as the nation's major city. Sarah Bernhardt, on her first visit, performed for adoring theater crowds and paid the city compliments: "Chicago is the pulse of America.

I adore it." She also took note of the ambitious nature of its citizens: "It is a city in which men pass each other without even stopping, with knitted brows, with one thought in mind—the end to attain."

Chicago had an intoxicating effect on Moses Bensinger. He moved his family there in the 1880s, took offices in a State Street building and frequented the company's factories, one at Rush and Kinzie and the other at Huron and Sedgwick. The latter structure covered an entire city block; it contained a factory, warehouse, and lumber-drying plant built in stages from 1881 to 1883 at a cost of $168,165 and designed by the famous architect Louis Sullivan.

That is where Moses Bensinger put his son to work in 1885. Benjamin Bensinger was 17 years old then, a recent high school graduate. He began work as a clerk, filing order forms in the dark and musty warehouse. At nights he attended Bryant and Stratton Business College.

Shortly after John Brunswick's death in 1886, Moses formed a separate firm, the Bensinger Self-Adding Cash Register Company, and put Benjamin to work there as a salesman. He was taking no chances. There was no assurance that Moses would become President of Brunswick, as Hugh Collender had taken that position after John Brunswick's death.

But when Collender died in 1890 and Moses did take over as President he ended his association with the cash register firm and brought his son Benjamin back to Brunswick. Though Balke's son, Julius Jr., and John Brunswick's son, B. H., remained executives with the firm, neither would play important roles. And through the 1890's most corporate observers correctly assumed that Benjamin Bensinger was the most likely heir to the company.

Indeed, through his steady and determined climb up the corporate ladder, Benjamin was obviously being groomed to one day take the reins from his father. By 1896, the year he married Chicagoan Rose Frank, Benjamin was a manager in the company's Chicago offices, making the lordly sum of $200 a month, a salary higher than all but a couple of crack salesmen.

"My father was not happy making any except the finest quality goods," Benjamin once told a reporter. "We were a shirt-sleeve organization. Our doors were wide open, physically and mentally—as nearly as we could keep them that way—to any one with a case to state. I remember the great pains my father took to see that we were open-minded. He was personally acquainted with every employee in the business, and it was a fairly big business even then."

Horse drawn wagons delivered goods from the impressive Brunswick factory. Covering an entire city block north of the Chicago River, the building was designed by famous architect Louis Sullivan and completed in 1883.

Muskegon, Michigan, was a quiet town when Benjamin Bensinger decided to build a new factory there in 1906. An original 100,000-square-foot structure, as seen below in the 1920s, would eventually grow into a million-square-foot manufacturing plant.

At the time he assumed the company's presidency following his father's death on October 15, 1904, 36-year-old Benjamin headed a prosperous firm, with sales offices in a half-dozen American cities and in Canada and Mexico; there were manufacturing plants in Chicago, Cincinnati, Dubuque and New York. Because he anticipated great growth in the years ahead, Benjamin immediately began planning for the building of a major new manufacturing facility. As soon as news spread that the aggressive company was looking for a new home, Benjamin was deluged with attractive offers from cities throughout the Midwest.

Grand Rapids, Michigan, was especially persistent and made a persuasive pitch. And then, into Benjamin's office walked Charles Hackley and Thomas Hume, two convincing boosters of Muskegon, Michigan. They came prepared.

Having thoroughly researched the company and its needs, they sat down and talked for 30 minutes without interruption. Rattling off a mind-boggling series of facts and figures, they came on like a couple trying to marry off their homely daughter.

In a sense they were. Muskegon at the time was a tough sell. It was a homely town, desperately in need of a prosperous mate. It was little more than an overgrown village of less than 25,000 people. Its streets were paved with sawdust and cedar, its buildings and businesses shabby remnants of the days when the city had been a lumber boom-town known as "Sawdust City."

But, sitting 160 miles across Lake Michigan from Chicago, Muskegon would make a perfect stopping-off point for company-owned boats that carried cut maple from the company's lumber mill in Big Bay, Michigan, on Lake Huron; wood which, in turn, came from the 1,000 acres of timberland the company owned near Lake Superior. Added to the desirability of its location was an ample work force.

Benjamin found the city most suitable, and on October 15, 1906, the company formally opened its 100,000-square-foot plant in Muskegon. One hundred newly hired employees and various local dignitaries gathered for the ribbon cutting ceremony. In charge of the operation was 29-year-old Fred Loewe, formerly an assistant to John Shank, production superintendent of all Brunswick plants.

Loewe was pleased with his new position, though he later remarked that when he and his family first arrived by train they had found Muskegon so unattractive "that we did all we could not to get back on the train." It was hard for him to imagine much excitement in this comparative backwater. He could not know that for the next 60-some years Muskegon would be the home of the company's most important plant.

Loewe looked around the opening day crowd until he spotted George Becker, supervisor of the billiard table assembly department, and J. O. Matteson, who headed the ball and chalk departments. They traded grin-and-bear-it shrugs.

T he Light That Never Fails. As far as advertising slogans go, it is not particularly catchy. When you consider that it concerns an item that has nothing whatsoever to do with light, the phrase seems not only of dubious value but suspect effectiveness. But Benjamin Bensinger liked it.

"Let's go with it," he said in 1906, and his salesmen went out to sell a revolutionary rubber bowling ball dubbed the Mineralite. It was the invention of Michael J. "Dad" Whalen, a man whose zeal for inventions perfectly matched Bensinger's taste for new products.

Ships loaded with cut maple from Brunswick's lumber mill were frequent visitors to Muskegon's docks.

Our Up-to-Date Continuous Bowling Alleys,
Equipped With
Simplex Pin Spotters
Were used at the
Big Paterson
N. B. A. Tournament
March 9 to 30, 1912.

The "Light" that never failed.

MINERALITE

Perfectly Round, Evenly Balanced
Cannot Warp, Shrink, or get out of True.
Used By All Expert Bowlers.

IMPROVED BACKUS PIN SETTER.
ALL METAL SUPPORT, CHAINS, ETC.
The Latest and most satisfactory
Pin Setter on the market.

The Brunswick-Balke-Collender Co,
Offices and Salesrooms: 29-35 West 32nd St., N. Y.

The Mineralite vied for attention in this announcement with a less successful innovation, the forgotten Backus Pin Setter.

Though the American Hard Rubber Company of New York actually beat Brunswick's Mineralite to market by a few months, when the company unveiled its "Indestructible Hard Rubber Ball," the Mineralite proved far superior and quickly took the lion's share of the market, boosting bowling's popularity. It was vermillion in color and retailed for $20. That was a lot of money at the time, but the ball was guaranteed to hold its shape for three years, was chip-proof, and provided a consistency that made the old *lignum vitae* balls obsolete. It was also the first major success of the "rubber men."

Since the 1850s, Brunswick had been studying rubber and its uses, employing scientists to conduct experiments with the elastic substance. These generally eccentric fellows came to be known collectively as the "rubber men," and though they made minor improvements on billiard cushion patents, their work was relatively insignificant.

Whalen changed all that. While overseeing the production of the Mineralite at the company's Muskegon plant, he continued to experiment. Bensinger adored him. Giddy over the immediate success of the Mineralite ball, he became intrigued with rubber and its potential uses. He gave Whalen a free hand, often sending him letters full of ideas.

One night in 1912, after dinner at his Chicago home, Benjamin Bensinger sat brooding over an editorial he was reading. He crumpled the paper and threw it across the room. He was frustrated. At a time of unprecedented growth and expansion, the clouds of moral outrage again shadowed one of Brunswick's principal products and he didn't like it.

Billiards, bowling, and bars had a long history of conflict with America's moral arbiters. The two sports had each been able, thanks in large part to Brunswick's constant public relations efforts and its unassailable quality in materials and workmanship, to flourish in spite of repeated outcries against them. But bars—they were a different story. Benjamin sensed, in the vitriolic editorials he was reading, that the latest attacks against the evils of drinking were more serious than those of the past.

The cry for the banning of the sale, manufacture, and transportation of alcohol had begun in the early 1800s, intensifying during the reform movement of the 1830s and 1840s. In 1846, Maine passed the first state prohibition law. By 1855, 12 more states had followed suit. But support for the cause waned during the Civil War. The Prohibition Party, founded in 1869 in Chicago, was unable to compete politically against the established parties. The Women's Christian Temperance Union, founded in 1874 in the Chicago suburb of Evanston, was the first important national prohibition group, but it was limited by the political weakness of women.

The movement gained new momentum with the 1906 formation of the Anti-Saloon League, a group of prohibitionist preachers, teachers, and businessmen. Its growth was rapid, its influence national, and its political action intelligently managed. It was an

American ingenuity on the move: the revolutionary Mineralite bowling ball embarking on a world tour in 1914.

unpleasant movement, tinged with bigotry and fueled by antipathy to the growth of cities, the presumed scene of most drinking.

As the attacks intensified, Brunswick launched a campaign to persuade voters that prohibition was a bad idea. It wasn't working. Some papers, such as the *Montreal Observer,* lambasted the company:

"The Brunswick-Balke-Collender Co., of Toronto, whiskey concern, has issued an enormous poster for the guidance of newspapers and voters. According to this poster, which has been sent to nearly all the papers in Canada, it is wrong for voters to vote for prohibition. Whiskey makes trade and gives people work and for this rea-son, asserts the poster, the voters should see to it that their candidate does not favor prohibition. The temperance sentiment is growing so strong that the whiskey makers have become thoroughly alarmed and are using every possible means for the influencing of the public against the destruction of their business . . . Rather does it influence all good citizens to so vote as to compel your directors, even against their own inclinations, to earn a living by some means not harmful to the body politic."

That sort of stinging response was not exclusive to Canada,

where prohibition laws were finally adopted in 1915. A growing number of American newspapers expressed similar sentiments, though rarely in such terms.

Brunswick continued to fill orders for its bars and a number of related accessories and fixtures such as beer glass shelves, bottle cases, railings, gates, food and beverage coolers, lunch counters, and window screens. But Benjamin Bensinger grew pessimistic and in preparation for what he felt was the inevitable, he began cutting back on production of the lavish and expensive bars.

Over three icy days in 1912, workmen began loading on trains Brunswick's considerable stock of fixtures in Kansas City. Sales had almost ceased there because of the prohibition movement, and the goods were to be moved to Chicago, where sales remained fairly strong.

An enterprising reporter from the *Kansas City Star,* a staunch advocate of prohibition, chanced to see the fixtures and bars being loaded for their trip north. He spent days digging up what facts he could. His story, claiming that Brunswick was running scared, caused considerable panic. Most of the country's tavern owners wanted to believe that prohibition would never arrive, and they looked to Brunswick as the most

knowledgeable source, and reliable barometer, on the issue. The story out of Kansas City caught everyone off guard and though prohibition was still nine years off, for all practical purposes Brunswick was out of the bar business.

"We eventually disposed of all our stock without loss, but it would have been the plainest folly to go on manufacturing more in that line," Bensinger later recalled. "We discontinued manufacturing bar fixtures at once and immediately looked around for some other business. . . ."

The Brunswick catalogue contained such practical items as this lavish beer cooler and such playful items as these decorative mirrors.

5

A Taste for Innovation

As billiards boom, Brunswick enters the prosperous but precarious automobile and music businesses

It was the tremendous popularity of billiards that enabled Benjamin Bensinger to enter such new fields as the manufacture of automobile tires which were emblazoned with the company's initials.

After nearly 70 years of unbridled success, Brunswick faced its first crisis when the prohibition movement knocked out the bar and bar fixture business. With it went $4 million in sales, nearly one-fourth of the company's annual revenue.

Some executives might have headed for the nearest tavern or highest window ledge. Benjamin Bensinger had a different idea—to quickly find a new business which might best utilize the company's existing manufacturing facilities.

The company was by no means in a dire situation. It was making not only billiard tables, but balls and cues and other equipment;

bowling balls and equipment; a complete line of church furniture, and the interior wood trim for churches, banks and commercial buildings. And the irrepressible Whalen was keeping things percolating in Muskegon. Benjamin sent Whalen notes filled with his observations on Chicago streets. Just as his grandfather had noticed the potential of the carriage trade on the streets of New York, so Benjamin had begun to think highly of the automobile business.

Cars careened all over Chicago streets. The city's first automobile club was formed in 1906, and by 1909 the Sears, Roebuck and Company mail-order catalogue was

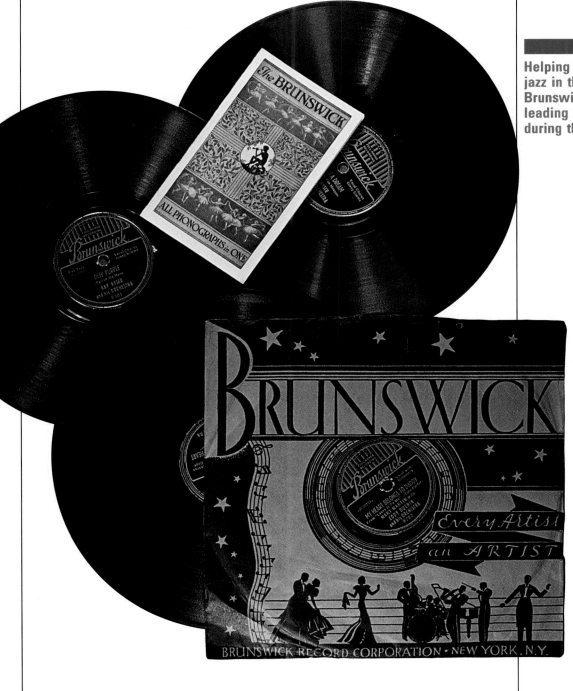

Helping to keep the jazz in the Jazz Age, Brunswick became a leading music maker during the 1920s.

trumpeting its "Motor Buggy . . . a practical car for use every day in the year over rural and city roads." The price: $395.

Whalen responded. A group of engineers under his charge made the first Brunswick tire in 1912. Actual production, however, did not begin for four more years since Whalen was onto something in which he saw greater potential than tires. That something was toilet seats.

In 1912, the company introduced its Whale-Bone-Ite, the first rubber toilet seat. It was a sensation. For a country accustomed to the rigors of wooden toilet seats, the Whale-Bone-Ite was greeted with almost tearful gratitude. A major purchaser was the Pullman Company, the nation's largest manufacturer of railroad passenger cars. Hotels unabashedly advertised, among their classiest amenities, "the comfort of the new toilet seats." Hospitals, offices, schools and government

buildings were eager customers. As Americans breathed a collective sigh of relief, production of the seats quickly reached a peak of 120,000 a year.

The tire business could wait. Bensinger felt no urgency to enter that market. At first, it seemed too modest. In 1914, there were only 1.3 million cars on America's dusty roads. Instead, he looked for other ways to use the men and machines idled by the cessation of the bar furnishings business. He considered many, from an expansion of the company's furniture line to building automobile bodies.

It was an employee in the company's Chicago factory who offered the first solution: piano cases. It seemed perfect. The cases called for the highest skill in the woodworker's craft, and there was no American company more renowned for its art with wood. The cases could be made in the company's factories without much adjustment. They could be sold in large

Invented by J. "Dad" Whalen and the "rubber men" in Muskegon, the Whale-Bone-Ite was America's first rubber toilet seat.

quantities to piano manufacturers, which would mean only a slight reorganization of the company's sales force.

The plan was put into action. Aided by the company's record for quality production, orders quickly reached sufficient number to keep nearly all of the under-employed woodworking facilities busy. Unfortunately, two years later, the piano business slumped badly and the company was back at square one. Bensinger, who put great faith in his employees and in plain thinking, instructed his sales force to look through newspapers and determine from advertisements what might be a fertile growth industry for the company. It was a deceptively simple strategy.

"Look through the newspapers, boys," Bensinger said. "And find me something we can make."

That something was phonograph cabinets. "We wrote a letter one morning to all the principal phonograph manufacturers asking if they would be interested in bids on phonograph cases," Bensinger recalled, as refreshingly matter-of-fact as if discussing a trip to the barbershop. "They knew of our work in the old lines and more particularly of our work in piano cases during the last years. Out of that letter and some brief negotiations came an order for $1 million worth of phonograph cases."

The company's principal client for the cases was the Edison Phonograph Company. And its timing was perfect, for a dance mania swept the land. Under the heading "New Reflections on the Dancing Mania," a magazine called *Current Opinion* declared in childlike wonder: "People who have not danced before in 20 years have been dancing, during the past summer, afternoons as well as evenings. Up-to-date restaurants provide a dancing floor so that patrons may lose no time while the waiters are changing the plates. Cabaret artists

Brunswick's craftsmen used their woodworking skills to create phonograph cabinets both handsome and functional.

are disappearing except as interludes while people recover their breaths for the following number. One wishes either to dance or to watch and to criticize those who dance." Record sales soared as tangos, one-steps, hesitation waltzes, and turkey trots came flowing off the presses.

Though the demand for phonographs was exceptional, Bensinger was not particularly pleased. Instead of patting himself on the back, he asked himself how he could make the best of a good situation. Finally it hit him: Brunswick should begin making and selling its own phonographs.

That idea made the company's executives nervous.

"Are you sure?" one asked him. "Don't you think it's a bit foolhardy to give up what's become a very lucrative line for . . . for what? Do we know how to make phonographs?"

"Someone in this company must know how to make one of those things," Bensinger said with typical confidence. "You've seen them. How hard could they be to make?"

He pushed ahead, motivated by what he felt an affront to the traditions of the company. "We were making cabinets in our own best style, and they were sold under a trade name not our own," he explained. "Cabinets were the most difficult part of the phonograph to manufacture, and the salesmanship of machines centered most heavily on aesthetics. It was the style and quality of the cabinets, rather than their tonal quality, that was most important to the first generation of phonograph buyers. We were building good will, so far as this line was concerned, only with a few manufacturers and not the general public. This was a far different situation than with our plan with billiard tables, bar fixtures, and the rest."

Furthermore, sales initiative in the line was largely in the hands of others. Whatever fine ideas Brunswick had for promoting the sales of phonographs were cannibalized by its customers, and not always to the best effect. These

The first Brunswick record was pressed in 1922, and it was followed by a steady stream of discs featuring many of the biggest stars and sweetest voices of the day.

were not the rules by which Brunswick liked to play. This was a company very uncomfortable as middleman.

Bensinger started to search through the company for someone who might make a prototype of the Brunswick phonograph. He visited the company's various factories. At the large plant in Muskegon he came across two fellows who expressed interest in the project.

"Have you ever made one?" Bensinger asked.

"How hard could it be?" they answered.

Benjamin Bensinger admired that sort of confidence. He had an insatiable appetite for new businesses and new products, and the sort of people who could produce them. He was always eager, in the days before research and development teams, to put free-lance inventors on his payroll.

"Here's $50," Bensinger told the two eager phonograph makers. "Go into town and buy whatever you need and build a couple of different models. When you're finished, send them to me in Chicago."

He returned to the company's offices in Chicago and waited. By April 3, 1916, the machines were ready. Surrounded by the members of the board of directors, Bensinger slowly rose from his chair and began to read: "There is the likelihood that the present contract with the Edison Phonograph Company will not be

Keeping the books was still a fairly simple matter as a distinguished-looking Benjamin Bensinger led the company through tremendous growth during the 1920s.

renewed . . . It was, after considerable discussion, decided to take up the manufacture of complete phonographs in two different styles."

At that moment, a pair of secretaries walked in toting the two experimental machines. They placed them at either end of the long table. Board members rose and surrounded the machines as if exploring toys on Christmas morning. A few minutes later, the phonographs were turned on and music poured through the room.

"I may have been prejudiced," Bensinger said. "But the machines didn't seem to work so bad."

On April 20, it became official: "This is an advance notice of our intention to put a high-grade

The cover of Brunswick's 1923–24 catalogue was adorned by elephants, while the inside contained page after page of equally impressive creations, such as the table below.

phonograph on the market," read a press release. "Samples together with advertising matter will be ready inside of sixty days. We expect to have the department in full swing considerably on the hitherto side of the holidays . . ."

"Our best quality machine, which will compare favorably with any high-grade machine on the market sold at $250, will list at about $150. This will be the same quality of cabinets that we are now producing for other makes of $250 machines. The tone arm and sound box will be gold plated. The motor will be Swiss-American, and best of all it will be provided with both Emerald or Black Diamond points, and regulation needles, so that it will play any of the four styles of records on the market . . ."

It was a good year, 1916, full of activity. As well as its new line of phonographs, Whalen and his "rubber men" were ready to put Brunswick automobile tires on America's roads. There was no way of predicting the future

of these new endeavors. But bolstered by the burgeoning popularity of billiards, Bensinger could afford to enter these precarious new fields.

The envelope contained a gold embossed brochure announcing the opening of Will Graney's billiard parlor in San Francisco. Benjamin Bensinger studied the photographs of the room's 42 tables. They were Brunswick tables, the finest ever made—sturdy and imposing, with intricate ivory inlays and mesh leather pockets festooned with gold tassels. Above them hung row after row of lights, and between them sat red leather club chairs, tables, and large, shimmering brass cuspidors. A smile lit Benjamin's face.

Make no mistake about his priorities. As voracious as he was for new products, Benjamin was keenly aware that billiards provided the financial foundation and solid reputation that enabled him during the 1910s and 1920s to venture into other businesses.

Billiards was his considerable bankroll. It is difficult today to comprehend how popular billiards was during the early decades of this century, especially when one realizes that until 1906, the game had a serious image problem.

It took a boy to change America's mind. Willie Hoppe was an ingenuous 18-year-old from Cornwall Landing, Long Island, when he sailed to Paris for a billiard match against Maurice Vignaux, then considered the greatest player in the world.

On the night of January 15, 1906, Hoppe stood across the table from Vignaux. They were playing to 500 points and the old master led, 266 to 228.

"The few Americans in the crowd didn't look too happy," Hoppe recalled. "The positions of the balls were marked with a pencil. The referee handed the ball to my father, who nursed it in his pocket throughout intermission to keep it warm. When we resumed, I kept close enough until I finally ran 93. That put me solidly in front at 417 to 295. I got the necessary 83 in two innings, one being a string of 75. When I went to bed that night I clutched a gold watch and chain and nearly $1,000 in cash, presents from my backers."

The next day, American newspapers headlined the victory of the "Boy Wonder." Hoppe returned to America a national hero. In Hoppe, America found the sort of virtuous young man any Bible belt mother could adore—a drab, non-smoking teetotaler who belied every commonly held image of the pool room denizen. The image of billiards began to change as Hoppe travelled throughout the country, giving exhibition matches in front of huge crowds. For him, it was work. For America, it was the beginning of a golden age in sports. In Detroit, fans filled the baseball park to witness the feats of a surly, talented rookie named Cobb. And they would soon be cheering the exploits of an ill-fated Indian athlete named Thorpe, a portly fellow named Ruth, a graceful tennis player named Tilden . . . and so many others. In less than a decade, American games were transformed from mildly amusing diversions into national spectacles.

Billiards was as popular as any sport. By the 1920s, there were more than 42,000 poolrooms in the United States, 4,000 in New York. In other cities, lavish parlors became minor urban landmarks and tourist attractions. One could play on the 42 tables at Ling and Allen in Kansas City, Sol Allinger's 37 tables, or the 70 tables at Hudson Recreation Center in Philadelphia. They could rack them up at Pope Sibley's 30 tables in Seattle or the 88 tables in the W. P. Mussey poolroom in Chicago's Loop. And how about the 142 tables in Detroit's Recreation?

After returning from his triumphant win over billiard master Maurice Vignaux in Paris, the straight-laced Willie Hoppe toured America and gave a jolt to billiards' popularity.

Jim Thorpe, shown in his football outfit, and Ty Cobb were among the talented athletes who turned America's sports from mere games into national spectacles.

At the Graney in San Francisco, one could mingle with socialites and hustlers in the Billiard Academy, a backroom playing area with a 400-seat spectator gallery—the nation's first, last, and only billiard casino.

Along with these great halls came a generation of famous players. They were household names—Hoppe and three-cushion stars like Augie Kiekhefer, Charles Peterson, Johnny Layton, and Bob Cannefax; pocket-billiard players like Alfredo DeOro, Emmett Blankenship, Frank Taberski, and Erwin Rudolphe.

The best and the brightest was Ralph Greenleaf. Unlike Hoppe, Greenleaf was a born showman, a fast-living and supremely talented player, a virtual model of Jazz Age attributes. He won his first title in 1919, held it for six years, and continued to win it on and off, until capturing his fourteenth crown in 1937.

Between tournaments he and his wife, the equally exuberant Princess Nai Tai Tai, toured the Orpheum vaudeville circuit, making as much as $2,000 a week putting on trick shot exhibitions on a table over which hung huge mirrors that gave the audience a view of the entire playing surface.

By the end of the 1910s, Brunswick was selling tables as fast as they could be produced at its eight factories in the East and Midwest. Chicago had become the company's official executive headquarters in 1908, when it dissolved its Ohio Corporation and incorporated in the state of Delaware. Its sales headquarters were in Muskegon, from where it ran a dealer network of 27 U.S. offices, five in Canada, plus overseas showrooms in London, Paris, Buenos Aires, Honolulu and Mexico City. Brunswick owned more than a thousand acres of hardwood timberland near Lake Superior, including a saw mill, lumber camp, general store, boarding houses, repair shops, a small railroad and steamboats to carry the lumber from its Big Bay landing to Muskegon.

The company owned its own slate quarries in Vermont and Pennsylvania. It was the world's largest user of hardwood. Its annual output of cues alone was more than 400,000, and it had enough reserve maple in its drying kilns (which were also the world's largest) to make an additional 600,000.

Any self-respecting billiard parlor proprietor filled his parlor with Brunswick tables, and the company was continually expanding its line to meet the various needs of its customers. The choice was wide. From the more than 15 models offered, one could choose the medium-priced Madison (1,950 pounds and finished in mahogany with white holly inlay, black border, and eggshell gloss), the Regal, the Regina, or the Sterling. And there was the majestic, top-of-the-line Arcade, a six-legged wonder of 2,760 pounds.

Brunswick's tables and equipment were the latest word in playing appointments. And its po-

sition of leadership in the business enabled it to direct official tournament billiards in the United States from the 1880s until the 1970s. For a time, it even owned copyrights on the official rule and record book.

Brunswick's determined effort to make billiards respectable for the middle class is dramatized by this persuasive advertisement from the Saturday Evening Post.

The young and stylish Duke Ellington was among the brightest stars on the Brunswick label.

It was Al Jolson, in his most famous pose, who made company cash registers ring with his best-selling "Sonny Boy."

The biggest-selling record of late 1919 was a catchy little song called "Alice Blue Gown." It was being played on many of the more than 2 million phonographs turned out that year by 200 American manufacturers. Four years earlier, there had been only 18 phonograph makers. But as the 1920s began, customers were jamming into stores, falling over themselves to buy the latest models.

Brunswick's phonograph business, which had shown an $18,000 loss during its first year, 1916, turned a handsome $703,000 profit three years later. Workers at the Muskegon plant could be heard whistling as production reached 750 phonographs a day.

Muskegon was a hotbed of activity. By 1921, with 10.5 million autos in the country, Brunswick was making more than 2,000 tires a day in Muskegon. But the com-

pany was but one of more than two dozen fighting for a share of the market. It became increasingly difficult to keep pace with those companies that had concentrated technology and better focused marketing strategy. The company might have been able to slug it out for a while, but when the price of rubber nearly tripled in 1922, Bensinger was left with no choice but to reluctantly discontinue the tire operation.

It was a pleasant surprise, and an indication of the company's name in the marketplace, when B. F. Goodrich approached the company for the rights to produce a tire under the Brunswick name, which it did the following year, forming the Brunswick Tire Corporation.

This experience soured Benjamin Bensinger on the rubber business and compelled him to boldly take the company further into the music business. Among the many reasons was that he did not enjoy listening to someone else's records spinning on Brunswick machines.

In order to make its own music, the company set up studios in New York. In January 1922, the first disc under the Brunswick label was pressed. An impressive collection of recording stars were soon signed to exclusive contracts—Duke Ellington, Benny Goodman, Cab Calloway, Montana Taylor, Red Nichols and his Five Pennies, and the wonderfully named Speckled Red and Cow Cow Davenport. The "Brunswick Hall of Fame" label signed such major classical performers as Richard Benelli, Mario Chamlee, Irene Pavlovska, and Leopold Godowsky.

This new industry proved extremely volatile and highly competitive. But Brunswick was a seasoned marketplace fighter. When the upstart radio industry threatened the phonograph business, the company responded quickly and began selling radios, forming an agreement in 1924 with the Radio Corporation of America to install RCA's popular Radiolas in Brunswick phonographs. RCA was at the forefront of a mushrooming industry. In Chicago in 1924, there were 30,000 receivers and a dozen radio stations.

And still more. In 1925, Brunswick collaborated with the General Electric Company to produce an all-electric phonograph. Called the

The ebullient Cab Calloway made beautiful music for Brunswick.

Panatrope, it came in various models (with or without radio) for $350 and up. It was a revolutionary item, the first electric phonograph on the market, and for it Brunswick and GE developed a new system of electrical recording.

Things could not have been more exciting, and the future could not have looked brighter. By 1928, Brunswick's sales topped $29 million. Emotions were running so carefree at corporate headquarters that when Al Jolson's 1929 Brunswick recording of "Sonny Boy" topped the pop music charts, the singer was made a member of the company's board of directors.

6 *Surviving the Storms*

The Depression rocks Brunswick, but Bob and Ted Bensinger preserve the company and enable it to respond to the War Effort

Taking over the company presidency in 1930, Bob Bensinger was determined to bring modern management methods to Brunswick and lead it boldly into its second century.

Robert Frank Bensinger, the eldest son of Benjamin Bensinger, was a handsome, successful, and generally happy young man as he sat down to breakfast at his home in the Chicago suburb of Glencoe one morning in the late 1920s. He read a story in the morning paper. It was an amazing story: Chicago teachers were being paid in scrip. This was the latest in a series of bad economic signs that peppered the morning papers.

In many ways Bob Bensinger felt beyond harm. The recent ripples in the American economy—the huge drop in housing starts, the inability of municipalities to meet their bills, the rising unemployment—did not seem likely to affect Glencoe. And Brunswick was thriving.

He could not have known that the disturbing stories in the papers were harbingers of the Great Depression. He had little experi-

They helped build airplanes and they helped keep things humming at Brunswick's plants. At the outset of World War II, women joined the workforce in great numbers.

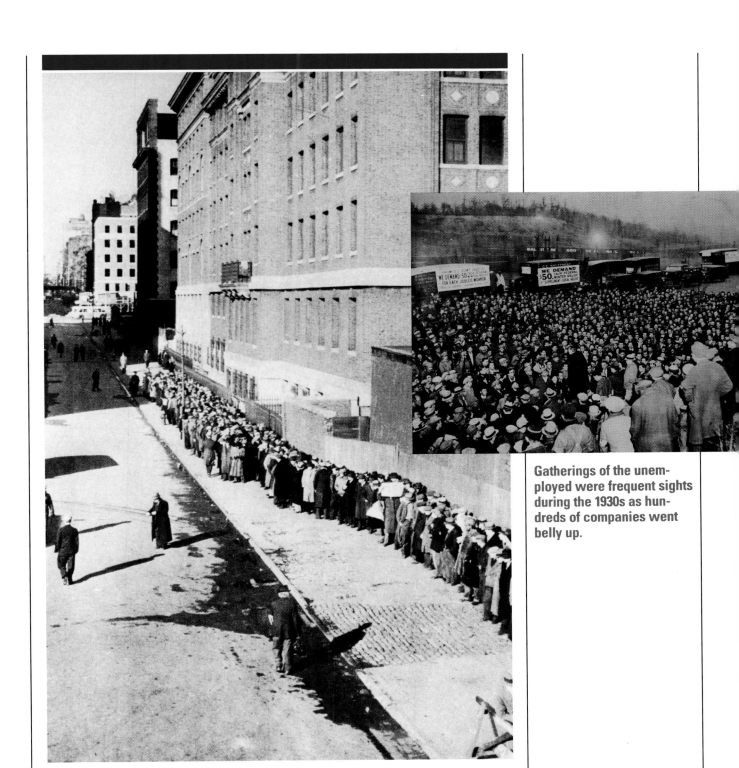

Gatherings of the unemployed were frequent sights during the 1930s as hundreds of companies went belly up.

ence with trouble, economic or otherwise. Born on February 10, 1898, in Chicago, Bob was raised in considerable comfort, as was his younger brother Ted, born in 1905. Bob attended Lake Forest Academy in suburban Chicago, Phillips Exeter Academy in New Hampshire, and he had been headed for an Ivy League education when World War I interrupted. He enlisted in the Navy. Returning from sea in 1919, he went to work for Brunswick and his father.

"My father was a tough taskmaster," Bob recalled. "He was a wonderful man but didn't believe in spoiling his sons."

Bob's first job was in the Muskegon plant, sweeping floors. Later he drove horse wagons—fetching and loading lumber at the docks, toting it back to the factory, checking it, counting it. Near the end of his two year Michigan stay, he tried his hand at the family's oldest trade. Working alone, he spent a month building his own billiard table.

He was not unhappy when summoned back to Chicago for a position in the credit department. During the next few years, he worked in every department of the company, developing a facility for dealing with bowling and billiard customers, and learning to speak their hard-edged language. In 1922, he was elected to the Board of Directors and he became a Vice-President three years later.

In appearance he closely resembled his father, with dark hair, a firm jaw line, and deeply expressive eyes. And it was assumed that he would eventually take his father's place as the President of Brunswick. Thoughts of that future were often on his mind some mornings in 1929 as he pored carefully over the news in the morning papers, little aware of the storms the next few years would hold for himself and Brunswick.

Moving east, the 20th Century Limited carried Benjamin Bensinger and his son Bob to New York and a $10 million deal.

One night in 1930, The 20th Century Limited rode through darkness from Chicago to New York. Aboard the train were Benjamin Bensinger and his eldest son, Bob. They did not sleep. When they arrived at Grand Central Station their sleeping compartment was a shambles, spread with hundreds of pieces of paper. They gathered their work and headed for a meeting with Harry Warner, the president of Warner Brothers Pictures.

Warner Brothers was one company that seemed able to weather the Depression. Its revolutionary Vitaphone talkies, most notably "The Jazz Singer," were setting box office records across the country.

Early in 1930, Warner had approached Brunswick about acquiring its phonograph and recording businesses. Warner wasn't really interested in the machines themselves. Instead, he saw great advantages in owning a record line on which he could promote and sell Warner film stars.

Benjamin Bensinger, and no doubt Warner, too, knew that Brunswick was in a bad bargaining position. The company had gone public in 1924 and, like most companies at the time, it had begun paying huge dividends to shareholders instead of building a cash surplus. Once the Depression hit, the banks began clamoring for the $9 million Brunswick owed. "And my father hated to owe so much money," recalled Bob.

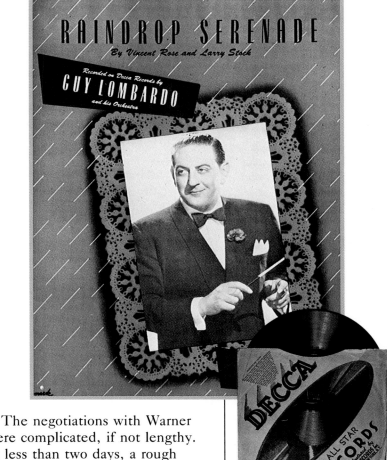

The negotiations with Warner were complicated, if not lengthy. In less than two days, a rough agreement was hammered out and, on April 9, 1930, a 42-page contract was signed. "I think it was the smartest deal my father ever made," Bob said years afterward. "It helped save the company."

What proved a good deal for Brunswick provided nothing but headaches for Warner Brothers. Two years later, in 1932, record sales fell to six percent of what they had been during the late 1920s, and Warner Brothers turned the Brunswick catalogue and trademark over to the American

Eventually many of the biggest Brunswick stars, among them Guy Lombardo, left Warner Brothers for other recording companies such as the aggressive new Decca label.

Record Company, a producer of bargain-priced 35 cent discs sold at Woolworth and similar chain stores. ARC continued to sell the more popular Brunswick performers on 75 cent records.

David and Jack Kapp, brothers who owned a small jazz record store in Chicago, changed that. Joining forces with a canny London stockbroker named E. R. Lewis, the Kapps formed Decca Records and persuaded most of the Brunswick "75 cent artists"

that they would sell more records, and lose no prestige, if they were on lower priced discs. Bing Crosby, the Dorsey Brothers, Guy Lombardo, the Mills Brothers and others joined the Decca label.

ARC was eventually purchased for $700,000, by William Paley, president of the Columbia Broadcasting System. Decca and the record industry flourished. Celebrating its fifth anniversary in 1938, Decca announced sales of 19 million records. Its "A-tisket, A-tasket" sold more than 300,000 copies, more than tripling the sales of former Brunswick board member Al Jolson and his "Sonny Boy." The value and reputation of the Brunswick label, however, was undeniable as its name continued to live on records into the 1950s.

The repeal of Prohibition in 1933 was the cause for many happy celebrations. It also prompted Brunswick to resume its bar and bar fixture business.

Warner Brothers paid roughly $10 million for the Brunswick Panatrope & Radio Corporation and, more importantly, "certain assets pertaining to the Musical Division." Using the money from the sale to pay off the company's bank loans, Benjamin Bensinger took the newly created position of Chairman of the Board and Bob took over as President. Through the dark days and uncertainty, Bob managed as best he could to keep the company alive.

"Things were very bad," Bob Bensinger said, recalling the Depression years. "We were forced to cut salaries three times in a period of two years. We tried everything not to eliminate people. We thought it better to cut salaries than let people go. But it was bad. We did eventually have to lay some people off. If we hadn't, we couldn't have survived. It hurt me so much, so very much."

Hundreds, even thousands, of companies did not survive the Depression. Chicago and its businesses were especially hard hit. By 1933, the number of people employed in the city was cut in half. Payrolls were down 75 percent. Foreclosures jumped five-fold, and more than 150 banks failed. Families evicted from their homes were living in the city's parks.

A godsend, of sorts, came in 1933 with the repeal of the 18th amendment and the company's guarded resumption of its bar fixture business. That industry had changed. No longer was there demand for expensive bars. Still, the company's tavern salesmen were greeted by tavern owners with the sort of affection usually reserved for fraternity brothers at a college reunion. The salesmen did not come empty handed. They offered a revolutionary table-top refrigerator called the "Blue Flash" and the response from institutional as well as home markets was enthusiastic.

Thus encouraged, the company began marketing a line of soda fountains in 1935. Though Brunswick had been making such items on a minor scale since the 1920s, the Depression had transformed the minor into major. The fountains were quickly followed by such items as the "Rubberceptor," a "leak-proof, safe, quiet, and sanitary" shower stall floor.

Brunswick's revolutionary Blue Flash—a table top refrigerator that was one of the company's most successful products during the 1930's.

The success of these goods was not spectacular, especially when compared to the profits of some of the company's pre-Depression products. But it was steady. It gave Brunswick financial breathing room, supplementing the greatly decreased cash flow generated by the sale of bowling and billiard equipment.

Though the thousands of pool parlors around the country were experiencing a boom, thanks to the tens of thousands of idle workers who found the rooms fine places to spend their time, the sales of new tables were virtually non-existent.

By the time Benjamin Bensinger died, on November 27, 1935, he had sadly watched his company shrink to the size it had been, and assume the general appearance it had at the turn of the century.

Company sales had fallen to a low of $3.9 million in 1932 from $29.5 million in 1928, and there was trouble collecting debts. During the early 1930s, the company's losses averaged $1 million a year.

One Chicago morning in the summer of 1938, a young man walked nervously south along Chicago's Wabash Avenue. Above him, the sun filtered through the wooden planks of the elevated train. Joseph Stefan watched his reflection in the windows along the street. It was just six blocks from the Marshall Field store, where he worked in the legal department, to his destination. But it seemed to be taking forever. Stefan had an 11:30 a.m. appointment with Julius Hoffman, a Brunswick

Though tavern owners were no longer in the market for the company's expensive back bars, Brunswick found the marketplace eager for its new line of soda fountains.

Vice President and General Counsel. Actually, the meeting was a job interview. He had heard from a former classmate at Northwestern University law school that Brunswick was actively recruiting "bright young men."

Finally, he stood in front of the company's 10-story building at 623 South Wabash. Stefan straightened his tie, buttoned his coat, took a deep breath and walked inside.

"I'll never forget it," he remembered years later. "It was . . . well, quite unbelievable. You must understand that I had been working at the Field building, and that it was a beautiful and very modern structure. The Brunswick place was something altogether different. The first thing I saw was a man in a cashier's cage, the old-fashioned sort, surrounded by wire. He was even wearing a green eyeshade. The elevators were open and rickety. Everything was so antiquated. Looking around that lobby for the first time I was tempted to turn around and run back to Field's. I felt like I'd stepped back in time."

The office of Julius Hoffman, who was later to gain fame as the federal judge presiding at the trial of a group known as the Chicago Seven, was on the fourth floor. Stefan's interview lasted more than an hour. Simpson E. Meyers, then head of the credit department, was also present.

"It was an intense session," Stefan said. "The company was eager to revitalize. It was seeking new

blood. The Depression had not been kind but the company was determined to fight back."

Leading the battle was Bob Bensinger, with the help of his younger brother, Ted. The brothers agreed that if Brunswick was to

The Studebaker Building on Chicago's Wabash Avenue became the Brunswick headquarters after a fire destroyed the company's previous home in 1913. Brunswick occupied the entire building until moving to more modern quarters in 1964.

be revived, it would have to undergo a major facelift, and so would the pastimes on which it depended. They ordered a management survey, the first in the company's history.

"It was an important move," said Bob. "We wanted a close look at weaknesses in individuals and

Remaining a leader in the recreation field, Brunswick filled orders for equipment from USO clubs and military centers, where troops got a chance for some relaxation.

departments. The report made a lot of recommendations. Some we followed, some not."

The effect was that of a general housecleaning. It led to the retirement of many executives and gave the company its introduction to modern management methods.

Brunswick's appearance in the summer of 1938 was deceiving. On the surface it had the shabby look of a battle-scarred survivor. But Stefan, and the many other "bright young men" visiting the offices at the time, were struck by the firm's energy and optimism. That is why, when Julius Hoffman stood up and said to Stefan, "We would like you to work for us," the young lawyer did not hesitate.

"Wonderful," he said.

"When can you start?" asked Hoffman.

"I've got to tell them at Field's and . . ."

"Well, the sooner the better," said Hoffman.

As the Depression eased and employment rose, poolroom attendance began to fall off for the first time in history. Initially, few at Brunswick noticed for there was a large, immediate demand for tables and equipment from a new source: USO clubs and military centers. World War II was on.

Brunswick was no stranger to defense production. During World War I, the company had supplied gun stocks and wooden wings for fighter planes. The company's first World War II government contract was for parachute bomb flares, used to illuminate areas during bombing raids. Other items followed: assault boats and aircraft fuselages, and floors and landing skids for Air Force gliders. B. F. Goodrich worked with Brunswick to supply self-sealing fuel cells for aircraft and floating mines. Brunsalloy, a lightweight but extremely strong metal alloy, was developed and used effectively as a substitute for aluminum in aircraft production.

From the plant in Muskegon poured these things and more: 60mm illuminating mortar shells, aircraft instrument panels, and aluminum litters. The plant easily handled the work, adapting smoothly from making the tools of play to fashioning the items of war; the place had grown, since 1906, into a one-million-square-foot operation.

Thanks to government contracts and the effects of its recent housecleaning, Brunswick was able to post sales of $20 million in 1942. Throughout the war, the company not only proved capable of making sophisticated products, but continued its dominance in the recreation field. By 1945, more than 13,000 billiard tables and 3,000 bowling lanes had been installed at military and naval bases here and overseas.

World War II took Brunswick permanently out of its Depression doldrums. It also signaled the emergence of Ted Bensinger as a force within the company. Ted's tireless work during the conflict had surprised many Brunswick executives since he had displayed only mild interest in the running of the company before that point.

Ted had joined Brunswick in 1928, a 23-year-old Yale graduate, recently married to Linda Galston, of Woodmere, New York. Like his brother before him, he began work in Muskegon.

Soldiers file into a huge glider for which Brunswick produced parts.

"We honeymooned for nine weeks in Europe. I caught a cold skiing in Switzerland and cured it on the Riviera," Linda Bensinger recalled. "It was glorious. And then we headed straight from the Riviera to Muskegon. It was 20 below when we arrived, and we stayed for two years."

Returning to Chicago in 1930, Ted was elected to Brunswick's Board of Directors, and during the Depression, he moved steadily up the corporate ladder: Assistant Secretary and Assistant Treasurer (1932), General Manager (1936), Executive Vice President (1937). He admitted that, for a time, he was more interested in taking "a lot of little vacations" than looking over ledgers. Those vacations, while they may have irritated some executives, did not bother Ted's brother, Bob. He knew that his family's passions extended beyond the executive office.

Their father, Benjamin, had loved to travel, making plant inspection trips to Europe, and often going to Africa, where he handpicked ivory for billiard balls. One of his favorite travel stories involved some ivory merchants in Amsterdam.

He went there every year, and was convinced that he was being swindled. The merchants spoke

French and Benjamin decided he would have to learn the language, too. He spent one year taking French lessons and when he returned to Amsterdam, he was ready. He listened calmly as the merchants began raising the bids they were making for him. After a few minutes he called them together and spoke to them calmly for a few minutes in perfect French.

"I was never cheated again," he said proudly.

On many of his overseas trips Benjamin was able to find time for things other than business, and some of Bob's and Ted's earliest memories were set in Europe.

Ted's lifelong fondness for foreign lands and adventure—he took bullfighting lessons in Spain, fished and hunted in the Andes, Alaska, and most places in-between—took a back seat when World War II began. He was very successful in gaining government contracts and became interested in the daily operations of Brunswick. It was as if he suddenly realized that even during war, business was business, and that there existed adventures aplenty in the board room.

Though 1945 marked the end of World War II with such euphoric scenes as this, it was also the year Brunswick celebrated its 100th anniversary, a long way from John Brunswick's cramped Cincinnati woodworking shop.

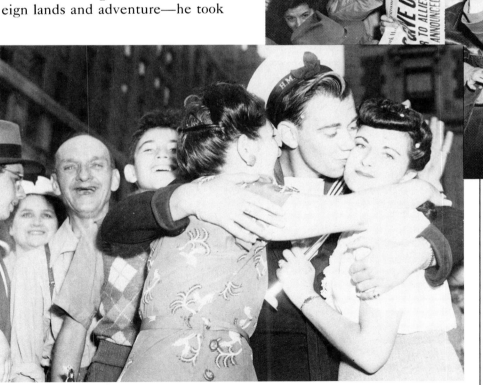

7 *The Pinsetter Wars*

Stunned by a rival firm's automatic pinsetter, Ted Bensinger works tirelessly to get a Brunswick machine on the market

The first shot in the Great Pinsetter War was fired by the American Machine and Foundry Company in 1946. At the American Bowling Congress tournament in Buffalo, New York, AMF stunned the bowling industry by unveiling an automatic pinsetting machine called the Pinspotter.

Brunswick did little but sit back and wait for the machine to fail. The general consensus in the industry was that it was impossible to create a machine that would pick up pins randomly scattered and put them back where they belonged every time.

As early as 1911, Benjamin Bensinger, his passion for new products and inventors in full flower, had put on the company payroll a Norwegian inventor named Ernest Hedenskoog in hope that he would one day make such a machine. Over the next three decades Hedenskoog managed to fill a Muskegon warehouse with all manner of strange contraptions and a trunkful of patents, but no pinsetter.

Not an inventor in the purest sense, Hedenskoog's desire to create an automatic pinsetting machine resulted from his dislike of pin boys. A precise man and avid bowler, he was forever at odds with them.

The passing of time has endowed pin boys with a charming image. They have become one of

The days of the pin boys, as shown in this 19th century illustration, were about to end as machines began to do most of the work on bowling lanes by the end of the 1950s.

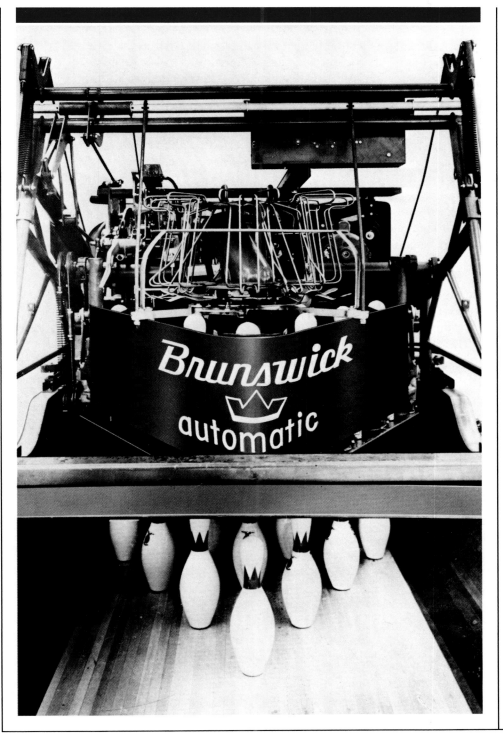

The sport of bowling would never be the same once the world was introduced to Brunswick's Automatic Pinsetter.

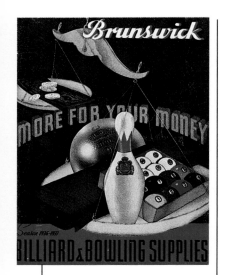

the icons of America's lost innocence. In reality, they were rarely boys, and few were noted for their charm. Their job was tough, back-straining work, an almost constant and dangerous game of tag with flying balls and pins.

"Before World War II," the New York Times reported, "many bowling places had reputations as hangouts for rugged characters who kept the air above the lanes blue with tobacco smoke and rough language; too many pin boys sassed back the customers or heckled the ladies."

Such types did not take lightly to abuse from Hedenskoog and, more often than not, ended his bowling games with fisticuffs. In 1919, he had come up with a magnetic machine able to pick up pins that hid a metal core. But the invention was far from foolproof. So, year after year, decade after decade, Hedenskoog continued to experiment in Muskegon.

Meanwhile, working in a henhouse at a friend's turkey farm in Pearl River, New York, another inventor named Fred Schmidt had developed and patented a vacuum device that seemed to solve the pinsetter puzzle. A jaunty Brunswick salesman named Robert E. Kennedy heard of Schmidt and his machine. Visiting the farm, Kennedy watched with fascination as Schmidt demonstrated his apparatus. On the spot the two men formed a partnership.

Kennedy first approached Brunswick with the project in the late 1930s. He was rebuffed.

"Who needed an automatic pinsetter?," Bob Bensinger remembered. "Not the bowling proprietors—they didn't have the money. Even if they did, why should they buy? There were plenty of pin boys around."

That was a decision he would regret. Kennedy went to AMF with his fistful of patents and a deal was immediately struck. AMF knew machines and sensed the pinsetter's potential. Founded in 1900 by Rufus Lenoir Patterson, the company revolutionized the tobacco industry by developing machines that weighed and bagged tobacco, and rolled and packed cigarettes and cigars. By the late 1930s, as AMF machines churned out a million cigars a year, Patterson's son Morehead was deliberately hunting for products to broaden the company. The automatic pinsetter filled the bill.

Nevertheless, it took AMF more than six years to produce what they believed to be a workable machine. It wasn't. The company's premiere 1946 machines displayed serious defects. They broke down frequently, and in a few months the machines were taken off the market. AMF went back to the research department.

Two years later, when AMF unveiled a second model, Brunswick began to market a semi-automatic device. Again, the AMF machine proved faulty and the company went back to the drawing board. Uneasily aware that AMF's persistence might eventually result in a workable machine, Brunswick hired Huck & Company, a small New York engineering firm, to evaluate all of the pinsetter development Brunswick had done over

Since being put on the company payroll in 1911, inventor Ernest Hedenskoog was determined to create an automatic pinsetting machine. Though his four decades of work failed to produce a practical model, many of his complicated patents provided the basis for what would eventually become Brunswick's Automatic Pinsetter.

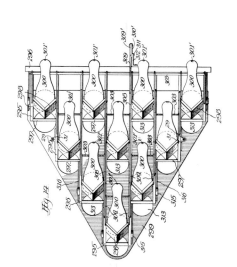

E. HEDENSKOOG.
AUTOMATIC PIN SETTING MACHINE.
APPLICATION FILED FEB. 13, 1914.

1,190,646.

Patented July 11, 1916
8 SHEETS—SHEET 7.

E. HEDENSKOOG.
MACHINE FOR SETTING PINS ON BOWLING ALLEYS.
APPLICATION FILED OCT. 28, 1914.

1,190,651.

Patented July 11, 1916.
9 SHEETS—SHEET 5.

Brunswick's line of school furniture was a big hit in the nation's classrooms after its 1953 introduction won the company a gold medal from the Industrial Designers Institute.

the years, including Hedenskoog's trunkful of dusty patents.

When Huck reported that Hedenskoog's contributions "contained the nub of a good device," Brunswick gave Huck the go ahead to make a prototype. Brunswick sent one of its employees, an M.I.T. graduate named Saul Jacobson, to New York to handle engineering responsibilities for the project. Unfortunately, money was tight. Though Brunswick's sales were $30.6 million in 1948, the company did not have the funds to

fully bankroll the project and banks were leery of investments in bowling.

The pinsetter project was put on hold while Ted Bensinger concentrated on other fronts. He was named President of the company in 1950 as Bob became Chairman of the Board, filling an office that had been vacant since Benjamin's death in 1935. Ted worked to round up new defense contracts during the Korean War, and he began looking for a new business that would broaden the company's product base. Howard Barber, in charge of corporate sales, was directed to find such products— items that would suit Brunswick's sales organization and manufacturing facilities. He decided on school furniture, and was given $1 million to develop a complete line.

Then AMF dropped a bomb. It displayed its latest Pinspotters in 1952 at Mt. Clemens, Michigan, and they worked.

"When we heard that, it was like a death pall hit the company," recalled a former Brunswick executive. "I was worried. Everyone was worried. I remember asking, 'What the hell are we going to do? Fold up our tents and walk away?'"

Ted Bensinger called Jacobson in New York.

"How long will it take you to get me a workable machine?" he asked.

"If we have the money we need?" said the surprised Jacobson.

"Yes, if you have the money," said Ted.

"I can get one in eight months," said Jacobson.

"Then get started," said Ted, unsure where he would get the many millions it would take to fund the project.

Jacobson and Huck developed a prototype in 1953 but the funds to go into production were still not available. That same year, the company's school furniture line was exhibited with spectacular success. Brunswick's entrance in this new field came at a perfect time, just as the first generation of baby boomers began filling new classrooms. Begun with the 1952 acquisition of Horn Brothers, an Iowa-based manufacturer and distributor of folding bleachers, partitions, and stages for school gymnasiums, this operation was bolstered by the redesign of several products and the addition of a line of classroom furniture designed through consultation with educators, architects, and orthopedic specialists.

The line was exhibited at a 1953 convention of the American Association of School Administrators. It was a smash. Within the year there were 47 exclusive dealers and agents handling customer demand in the United States and Central and South America. The Industrial Designers Institute awarded the new line a gold

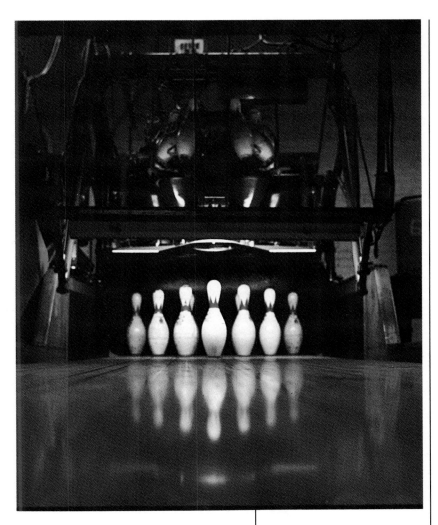

medal, the first time it had so honored school furniture.

Bolstered by that success, Ted restructured the company in 1953, forming seven operating divisions: bowling and billiards, school furniture, Horn, defense products, export and subsidiary operations, organization and distribution, industrial relations and personnel. He shifted executives, giving increased responsibilities to many of

This innocent looking member of the first generation of Brunswick's Automatic Pinsetters would not only change the sport of bowling, but alter the face of Brunswick itself.

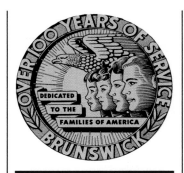

Anyone who thought Brunswick's first century had been exciting, hadn't seen anything yet, as the success of the Automatic Pinsetter made most past ventures seem tame.

"the bright young men" recruited during the housecleaning of the late 1930s.

Many of them played crucial roles during the Pinsetter Wars. Joseph Stefan aided Bensinger with the complicated legal matters of getting the Pinsetter produced. Lester Swanlund provided financial wizardry. Sid Meyers was tapped to head the bowling and billiards division.

And Ted rallied the troops. "Ted said that if we'd bust our backs and behinds and get in there and scratch, he'd see to it we'd all be well rewarded," Meyers recalled. "All he wanted was miracles."

His energy, however, failed to

impress the bankers, who turned down Brunswick's requests for loans. It was a chance meeting with Byron C. Gould, President of the Murray Corporation of America, that eventually led to the development of Brunswick's Pinsetter.

Murray had just lost a huge body-making contract with Ford Motor Co., and so Gould was in the market for something else. After talking with Ted, a match was struck: Gould had the money, a spare $20 million, and Brunswick had the "something else." Initially, Gould tried to buy Brunswick out of the project for $15 million. Ted would have none of that. Instead he orchestrated a remarkably good deal for his company—Brunswick supplied only the patents to its Pinsetter and Gould supplied $10 million.

"Only Ted's remarkable charm could have swung such a deal," an executive later noted. Others were equally impressed. In what one observer described as a "spontaneous welling up, like at a Quaker meeting," Brunswick's Board of Directors bestowed on Ted in 1954 the new title of Chief Executive Officer.

Brunswick and Murray formed the Pinsetter Corporation. A workable Pinsetter, manufactured by the Otis Elevator Company, was produced within a year and was ready for field testing in 1954. But Murray Corporation's cash involvement began to escalate above original estimates. By the time the machines were in production in late 1955, Murray had spent nearly $16 million. Gould demanded a renegotiation of the original contract and a bigger share of the revenues.

Ted didn't want that. The only thing he could do was buy Murray out. After a hurried conference with Harold J. Szold, a banker and Brunswick director, Ted approached the C.I.T. Financial Corporation and persuaded it to take a thoughtful look at the Pinsetter's potential. C.I.T. was impressed enough to award Brunswick one of the largest credit lines it had ever extended—$55 million.

Gould, unaware of this transaction, expected to get a bigger share of the pie when he arrived for a meeting with Ted at a Chicago bank.

"It was pure drama on Ted's part," recalled one who was there. "People were squeezed so tight in the room it was hard to breathe and here were all these Murray executives licking their chops at what they thought would be Ted's failure. When he appeared he was smiling like a little kid. He walked over to each of the Murray executives, shaking hands and making small talk. Sticking out of the front pocket of his suit was the end of a check. Finally, when Ted got to Gould, he took the check out and handed it to him. You should have seen Gould's jaw drop."

The check was for $18 million. Murray was out. The Pinsetter was Brunswick's.

8 The Bowling Boom

The spectacular success of the Pinsetter makes bowling a national rage and causes Brunswick's stock to soar

At the end of the 1950s, bowling had firmly captured the fancy of Americans of all ages, a custom-made delight that filled the lanes from coast to coast.

They laughed at us," said Milt Rudo, remembering the reaction of bowling proprietors to the news of Brunswick's Pinsetter. The son of a district manager in Brunswick's bowling operations, Rudo had joined the company in 1940, forsaking Harvard Law School for a career as a bowling salesman. As the Pinsetter Wars heated up, Rudo found himself in charge of 60 salesmen trying to hold the line against AMF's Pinspotter. At first, all they had to offer was Brunswick's reputation and a hastily devised slogan: "Worth Waiting For."

AMF had a huge lead. By the time Brunswick's machine was ready for installation in 1956, more than 9,000 of AMF's Pinspotters had been installed on the country's lanes.

Ironically, the Pinspotter owed much of its early success to Brunswick, which during the 1940s and 1950s had aggressively marketed bowling. It had introduced major design changes, streamlining lanes and adding flashes of color to them. On their way out were the old wooden spectators' benches; they were being replaced with comfortable chairs in a semicircular setting. Brunswick architect Edgar Lynch began designing colorful, cheerful-looking bowling centers.

Often by offering financial aid, Brunswick convinced many bowling proprietors to embrace these

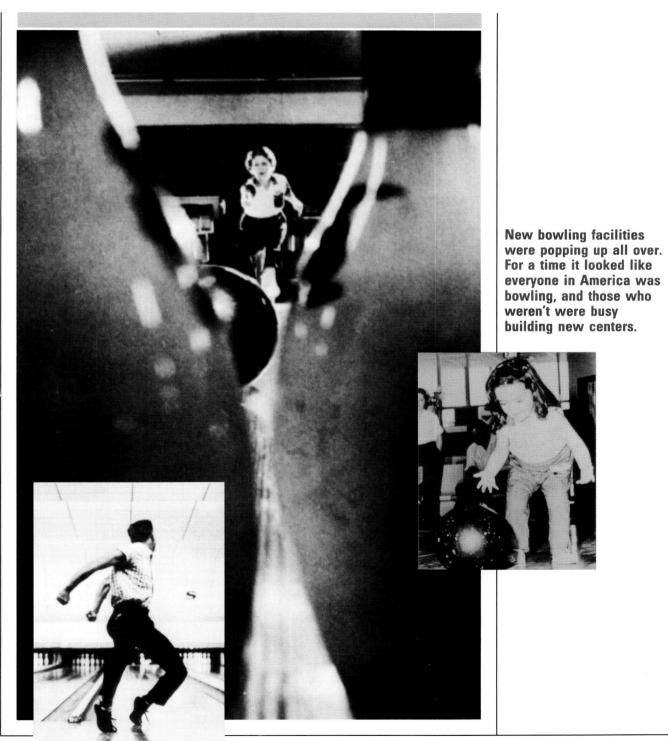

New bowling facilities were popping up all over. For a time it looked like everyone in America was bowling, and those who weren't were busy building new centers.

Don Carter and Marion Ladewig display the fruits of a couple of their many victories, providing ample reason why they were the leading members of Brunswick's professional bowling staff.

modern principles and create "recreation centers." It was a well coordinated and successful effort, and for the first time women were attracted to the sport in large numbers.

"Bowling's image was never as bad as that of billiards," recalled Bob Bensinger. "But it needed a little polishing anyway. What we did was bring a more pleasant atmosphere to the sport and women took to it like fish to water."

Women and men alike took to another Brunswick bowling innovation of the 1940s: balls with holes drilled to fit players' hands. These "customized" Mineralite balls were sold in department, jewelry, and even hardware stores. In 1947, the Muskegon plant turned out twice as many as the year before. The company also introduced a lightweight ball called the Junior Mineralite, along with a complete line of accessories for youngsters.

The updating of the sport's gear, the advent of modern interior designs, and the increase in the number of new players convinced many bowling center owners that the sport would grow in popularity. Most everyone, however, was stunned by the explosiveness of that growth. Along came the pinsetters, freeing owners and customers from surly and increasingly hard-to-find pin boys, and allowing centers to operate dozens of lanes at all hours without an army of casual laborers.

And the boom was on.

Sid Meyers had already proven himself in a variety of corporate roles when he was tapped in 1955 to take charge of the company's 125-man salesforce and bring the Pinsetter successfully to market. He had joined the company in 1936 as Credit Manager and became Export Division

Manager in 1939. He became a member of the Board of Directors in 1941, a Corporate Vice President in 1944, and Director of Foreign Operations in 1945.

He was a marketing master, and had to be. He was in a tough and often messy battle, fighting at first a war of words with AMF, which loudly maintained that Brunswick's Pinsetter was beset with problems and would never see market.

He was understandably nervous when, shortly after midnight one night in early April, 1956, four large trucks pulled up in front of the Roselle Lanes, a bowling center in Roselle, New Jersey. Throughout the night and early morning, dozens of workmen unloaded 16 large, cumbersome, and strange looking machines—Brunswick's Automatic Pinsetters.

For the next week workmen toiled furiously to get the machines installed . . . and working. At night, two hulking armed guards watched the premises as if protecting a secret military installation. Such was the bitter nature of the battle with AMF that sabotage was expected.

It had happened earlier in that year. Someone had gotten into the factory where the Pinsetters were being made and snapped pictures of the dismantled machines. One of those pictures found its way to AMF, which sent copies to bowling center owners around the country, accompanied by this pithy note: "This is Brunswick's

Automatic Pinsetter. Are you going to wait for this or buy AMF?"

The wait ended on April 10, 1956, when the Pinsetters made their official debut. It was a major sporting event, covered by dozens of reporters. One wrote in the *New York Journal American:* "With nary a single case of first night jitters, machines on all 16

At an early stage in the production process, here's one of the thousands of Pinsetters that came off the assembly line in Muskegon.

These magazine covers perfectly capture the thrills people were getting at their neighborhood bowling centers.

Milton Berle, one of TV's earliest stars, was also one of bowling's biggest boosters.

lanes did exactly what automatic pin-setting machines are supposed to do: they set wood in approved American Bowling Congress fashion, returned balls to their rightful owners, and gave signals via colored lights on an attractive masked unit. All this was done quickly and quietly . . . What more could be asked of a robot—even one that took more than two decades to develop?"

There was little time for jubilation at Brunswick. Of immediate concern was the task of filling more than $30 million in orders. Meyers and his sales team had done a remarkable job. A surprising number of bowling customers believed Brunswick's machine was indeed "worth waiting for." By the night the Pinsetter premiered, orders had already been received for more than 4,000. And at first, production was only a trickle.

"Just as we were all patting each other on the back for holding the line against AMF, we had to figure out how to fill orders for

machines we didn't yet have," recalled Rudo, who worked for Meyers at the time. "Who would we satisfy first? I started getting calls at home from people begging, screaming for their machines. I told them all the truth, that they would have to wait. I was amazed at how many stayed with us. This company had a lot of loyalty."

Loyalty, and a very good product. By the end of 1956, 2,000 Pinsetters had been installed. The next year, that number swelled to 7,000. By 1958 more than 11,000 Pinsetters were doing their work on America's lanes, and the number continued to grow, as if there was no end in sight.

Toward the understanding of the Pinsetter's impact on Brunswick, the following figures speak eloquently.

1954: Sales, $33 million. Earnings, $700,000.

1961: Sales, $422 million. Earnings, $45 million.

The view from company headquarters was stunning. It looked as if everyone in America was bowling, and those who weren't were busy building bowling centers. Brunswick, determined to solidify its stature in the industry, began to use television, sponsoring "Championship Bowling," a 1950s ratings smash and an effective marketing tool for the sport.

By the thousands Americans were drawn to the sport. In response to this increased demand, new and elegant bowling centers began to dot the suburbs, some costing as much as $2 million. They were air conditioned, with 80 or sometimes as many as 100 lanes. Some had built-in restaurants, cocktail lounges, snack bars and soda fountains, as well as billiard rooms. The more lavish centers offered swimming pools, meeting halls, and nurseries.

These places were called, generically and understandably, "Taj Mahals," but they took such names as Bowleteria, Bowlodrome, Bowlerama, and Bowlero. The largest was Edison Lanes in New Jersey, with 112 lanes side-by-side.

Bowling was fun, healthy, inexpensive, and, to most Americans, novel. Even a beginner could feel the rush of a strike, a brush with perfection. On a subtler level, the centers provided a social focal point for new, sprawling suburban developments.

Behind the scenes with the Pinsetter, these four nuns were captivated by the wonders of the machine.

Everyone wanted in on the action. Gil Hodges, Sherm Lollar, Stan Musial, Joe Garagiola, Yogi Berra, Phil Rizzuto and Mickey Mantle—all of these sports greats, and many others, were proud owners of bowling centers by 1960.

"Perhaps most remarkable is the success of proprietors in luring families into their premises—and the way in which women and children have embraced the sport," noted *Today's Health* magazine at the time. "Women bowlers now number six million (versus 82,000 in 1940), and more than a million of them take the game seriously enough to have joined the Women's International Bowling Congress. The American Junior Bowling Congress has grown from 8,700 boys and girls in 1946 to more than 185,000."

There were more than 100 magazines and newspapers devoted to the sport. Nearly 140 daily newspapers carried bowling columns. Most every metropolitan area had its own local TV bowling program, and bowling stars began to outnumber TV cowboys and private eyes. Brunswick had 60 men and women professionals working for the company and found it necessary to have employees working full-time filling the hundreds of weekly requests for the autographed pictures of such stars as Don Carter and Marion Ladewig's "Bowl to Stay Slim" brochure.

Riding the crest of this boom, Brunswick's stock soared. The company was the darling of Wall Street. Its stock increased spectacularly in value between 1953-59. This naturally thrilled stockholders and the Bensingers, who owned about 10 percent of the company's shares.

Most of the credit for Brunswick's good fortune was showered on Ted Bensinger. He became, to put it mildly, a superstar of the business world, and dozens of national magazines lavished praise on the man and the company.

Fortune, in its November 1959 issue, took a long and detailed look at both in "Brunswick's Automatic Money-Maker." *True* magazine gave them six pages in October 1960: "Ted Bensinger: He Found Profit in Play." *Time* magazine had its say late in 1960: "Ruddy and trim (6 ft., 170 lbs.), Bensinger likes sports and travel

Brunswick aggressively promoted the sport on television and on roadside billboards.

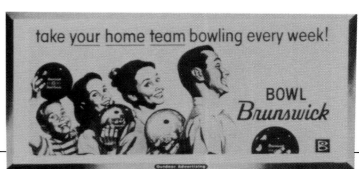

almost as much as his job. He has shot pigeons with Ernest Hemingway in Cuba, sipped wine with Pablo Picasso in Paris, played golf with Sam Snead . . . . He even finds time to bowl occasionally, once rolling a 286 game."

In a profile that makes current sporting-businessmen seem tame by comparison, *Sports Illustrated* devoted five full pages to Ted Bensinger: "The whole Brunswick complex as it exists at present is an extension of one man's astounding energy and drive; it is a monument to Bensinger and the American system of business management—and it is interfering with his duck calling." The December 25, 1961, article—a fine Christmas gift—went on: "Bensinger rides, hunts and fishes. He has fought bulls on Juan Belmonte's ranch and has run with them in Pamplona. He golfs and plays tennis and skis, shoots billiards, bowls, flies airplanes and, of course, calls ducks. In between, he goes to games to watch other people do things."

Ted lived with his wife, Linda, and their three sons, in a large, ivy-covered house in the Chicago suburb of Highland Park. It was there that Linda Bensinger recalled some of the changes wrought by the tremendous success of the Pinsetter. Three decades after the Pinsetter Wars, she sat on the sun porch, a room filled with color that looked out onto the ravine that cut a path through the area.

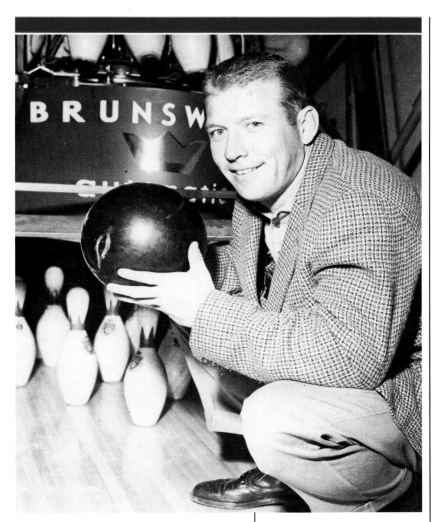

"There was a time when we had the most wonderful parties here," she said. "We would have all of the employees over. They would fill the lawn." She looked out toward a wide area of grass that stretched into the distance. "It was wonderful. So many nice people and Teddy knew everyone who worked for him. He tried to at least . . . then the company just got so big . . . so fast."

Everybody wanted in on the boom, and New York Yankee great, Mickey Mantle, was all smiles at the opening of his new center.

9 General Motors of Sports

Ted Bensinger begins the era of Brunswick's greatest growth by acquiring a number of recreation companies

The making of golf clubs became a new part of Brunswick's business in 1958.

Fueled by the success of the Pinsetter, Ted Bensinger developed big dreams for Brunswick, and in 1958, he began to act on them. He would spend the next four years on an incredible buying spree, acquiring 18 new firms of all size and stripe. In the process, he would transform Brunswick.

For more than 110 years, the company's growth had come strictly from internal business development. Bensinger was determined that Brunswick's future growth and diversification would come from acquisitions. Though his dreams would eventually not all come true, his vision took what had been basically a bowling and billiard firm boldly into the new fields that laid the foundation for the company as it is today.

"Ted wanted to make Brunswick into a conglomerate," recalled one executive. "The money generated by the Pinsetters made it easy for him to buy companies. Our stock was so golden that companies were lining up to become part of Brunswick in exchange for stock. Ted was a zealous buyer. It was an exciting time."

Growth through acquisition, though, can be a precarious game. There is no sure thing. Ted played it like a gambler on a hot streak, and he had plenty of backers. To board members and shareholders, Ted had a Midas touch. Most of them considered the success of the Pinsetter his

Union Hardware Company, acquired by Brunswick in 1959, had a long association with American sports, creating such items as this for 19th century skaters.

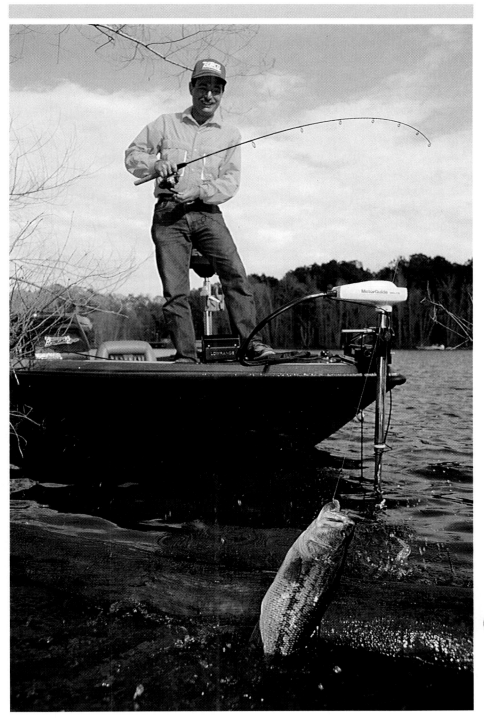

Zebco would prove to be one of Brunswick's most successful acquisitons, helping fishermen like this fellow catch the big ones.

1949 witnessed the start of a fishing revolution, when Zebco produced this *Standard* medel, the world's first spincast fishing reel.

victory; they credited his enthusiasm and energy with propelling the machine triumphantly to market. So, when he began to expand Brunswick, those around him generally let him have his way.

The most obvious facet of this expansion was Ted's desire to make Brunswick the "General Motors of Sports." He was often heard bouncing that phrase off his executives. They would understand and smile. There was something undeniably catchy about it and the grand idea it implied.

In 1958, Ted began to act, purchasing MacGregor Sports Products Incorporated, a leading recreational firm that fit his dream to eerie perfection. It had been founded in Dayton, Ohio, in 1834—the year John Brunswick arrived in America. At first MacGregor was in the carriage-making business; Brunswick was a carriage-maker. It took advantage of the late 1800s boom in American participatory sports to enter the golf business, as did Brunswick with bowling. Its headquarters moved to Cincinnati, Brunswick's founding city.

Such coincidences, however, had little to do with Bensinger's decision to buy the company in exchange for $6 million in Brunswick stock. Ted proudly an-

At the MacGregor Factory, the manufacture of golf equipment was an exacting process.

nounced that the acquisition gave Brunswick "the ability to serve the world in year-round recreation."

MacGregor manufactured a wide variety of sporting goods: balls for football, golf, baseball, and basketball; golf clubs, bags, and shoes; shoes and equipment for football and baseball; tennis balls and rackets, as well as gloves and uniforms.

"The purchase seemed like a good thing at first," recalled Joe Donatiello, who started work at MacGregor in 1937, sweeping floors in the shoe factory. "There were some adjustments to be made. But they painted our old factory building, and that was a welcome sign. The place was very old, dark, and dismal. The paint brightened things."

Donatiello was a foreman at the time of the acquisition. Over the next two decades and more he watched MacGregor grow and change, and not always for the best. "We were a family-type place," he said. "We were filled with a lot of old-timers who were used to working on a certain level. Once Brunswick took us over, we started to grow so fast. Old and new methods didn't always work well together. Sometimes they didn't work at all."

Moving further into the recreational field in 1959, Bensinger bought Red Head Brand, a 102-year-old company that was a leading manufacturer of outdoor clothing and equipment in the boating, hunting, fishing, and

Before bouncing across America, MacGregor basketballs were carefully crafted and built to last.

camping areas. In Red Head's 87,000-square-foot factory on Chicago's Northwest Side, the company also made fishing rod covers, piano and organ covers, voting booth curtains, and, since the 1920s, billiard cue cases for Brunswick.

Union Hardware Company of Connecticut, the world's oldest and largest maker of roller skates, soon joined the fold, along with its line of ice skates, shoes for bowling, football, baseball and track, and golf club shafts. The Royal Manufacturing Company of Ponce, Puerto Rico, also came aboard. Founded in 1952, it manufactured hockey, baseball, boxing, and football equipment.

Almost overnight, Brunswick became a sporting goods giant,

At the massive Owens factory in Baltimore, workers are shown in the process of creating a yacht.

distributing more than 5,000 products. A new, 166,000-square-foot plant was built in Eminence, Kentucky in 1960 to support and consolidate the manufacture of Brunswick's sporting goods.

Ted kept busy, taking the company into the recreational boating field with the 1960 purchase of the Owens Yacht Company, a leading manufacturer of fiberglass and wooden boats, from 25-foot cruisers to 45-foot yachts. The company's facility in Baltimore was the largest plant for boat production in the world. Almost simultaneously, Ted bought Larson Boats, a Minnesota manufacturer of small motor boats and canoes.

It was a wonderfully busy period (the company changed its name to Brunswick Corporation on April 18, 1960) and one that Ted relished. And no more so than on a brisk spring day that year, at the Annual Stockholders meeting at Chicago's South Shore Country Club. Before getting down to business, shareholders watched a putting contest between company directors and pros from MacGregor's advisory staff. This was the flamboyance Ted loved and many stockholders expected. The previous year, the shareholder's meeting had been held in a Chicago suburban school to highlight the company's school furniture line.

On the fairways of South Shore's golf course stood such golfing greats as Jack Burke and Louise Suggs, giving a special golf clinic. It was as if Ted and his brother Bob, who remained Chairman of the Board, were trying to provide a physical manifestation of the "General Motors of Sports" dream, something the stockholders could see and feel.

The stockholders were duly impressed: "I'll never forget it," said one stockholder, still wowed after more than two decades. "And you know what? Bob Bensinger hit the ball farther than any of those professionals."

What would prove to be the most important of Ted's recreational acquisitions took place in 1961, when he purchased Zebco. Based in Tulsa, Zebco had begun as the Zero Hour Bomb Company in 1932, making time bombs used to activate oil wells. It was in a different business by the time it caught Bensinger's eye. It had become a leader in the fishing tackle market with a line of closed-face fishing reels.

Zebco's remarkable transformation had taken place in 1949 when a west Texas native named R. D. Hull came looking for work. Instead of a resume, the watchmaker-inventor-fisherman carried in his hands what Harold Binfors, then Zebco's General Manager, referred to as "something that

looked like a beer can with a hole in both ends."

The contraption would revolutionize fishing. The very first Standard reels began rolling off production lines in June, 1949, followed by the sleek Model 22 in 1953 and then the classic Zebco 33. Incorporating the now-famous Zebco contoured thumb button and sensitive drag adjustment, it was America's first true closed-face spinning reel. It was followed by innovations and variations: the 44, made for improved American-type straight handle rods, and the 55, for heavy-duty fresh water fishing, surf casting, and spinning. In 1956, the Zebco name was adopted, and the Zero Hour Bomb Company, still active in the oil field accessory industry, became a division of the tackle firm.

Garbed in nautical attire, Ted Bensinger and Charles Owens happily formalize the deal which made the Owens Yacht Company part of Brunswick in 1960.

Thousands of closed-faced spinning reels rolled off the production line at Zebco's plant in Tulsa.

Ted Bensinger, joined by Japanese Consul General Takeo Ozawa and Mitsui representative Tetsuro Sanda, shares his high hopes for bowling's future in Japan, one of the many foreign countries eager to participate in the sport.

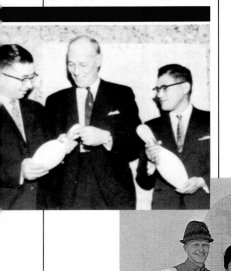

Thanks to the ease with which Zebco products could be used, America started turning on to fishing as never before. Unit sales at Zebco rose a stunning 280 percent from 1954 to 1957. The Tulsa plant expanded as sales and distribution grew from the immediate Tulsa area to embrace all parts of the U. S. and 27 foreign countries.

This spectacular growth did not go unnoticed by Ted Bensinger, a lifelong fisherman. He felt the company a perfect match for Brunswick and he hit it off immediately with Zebco's president, Ralph Lafferty. A charismatic man, Lafferty was revered by many of the employees at Zebco's tidy, homey plant in Oklahoma. He had a personal touch that Ted understood. Walking through the Zebco plant, Lafferty would often stop beside employee after employee, asking questions such as: "Rosie, how's your little boy?"

Lafferty and Zebco were introduced to Brunswick shareholders at the annual meeting in 1961. Some 5,000 of Brunswick's 75,000 shareholders were on hand, having made their way through the unseasonably snowy April weather to McCormick Place on Chicago's lakefront. They had walked through a lobby filled with 26 luxury yachts and fiberglass boats and displays of other company products. Inside, they sat happily while Bensinger provided a typically upbeat show.

He introduced Lafferty as "the newest addition to the Brunswick executive family." Lafferty's handsome face flashed onto a giant screen on the auditorium stage and the man himself bowed from the audience. Bensinger went on to announce that sales and earnings were going up.

A good portion of the afternoon's program was given to news of the foreign countries in which Brunswick and bowling were making inroads. The shareholders knew that in 1959 Brunswick had purchased a plant near Dublin to manufacture and assemble bowling equipment and that the next year, in partnership with Britain's Rank Organization, 20 movie theaters in England were converted to American-style bowling centers. Ted further informed them of the opening of Brunswick centers in Germany, Holland, Belgium,

France, Austria, Mexico, Peru, Sweden, Brazil, Italy, Switzerland, Finland, and Australia.

The European and Australian markets looked particularly promising for Brunswick and bowling. Few paid much attention to the news that Brunswick had, in 1960, entered the Japanese bowling market through the establishment of Nippon Brunswick, a joint venture in which Brunswick was an equal partner with Mitsui & Co. Ltd., a large Japanese trading company. Few could have anticipated the bowling boom that would eventually seize Japan or the importance of the Southeast Asian market in the coming decades. At the 1961 shareholders' meeting people were convinced that with Ted's leadership, the future would take care of itself.

Ted ended the proceedings with a bang: A 100-foot curtain parted to reveal a newly-designed Owens yacht, shining in floodlights and covered with attractive models in nautical garb. And a band began to play. "It was like a revival meeting or a Broadway opening," recalled one who was there. "It was smiles. It was magic."

10 Into New Fields

Time would prove that Ted Bensinger's entrance into the marine power would be among his wisest decisions

Operating rooms around the world were among the places Sherwood products were found.

The 1961 acquisition of Kiekhaefer-Mercury would surprise even its most optimistic principals.

The appeal of Ted Bensinger's recreational acquisitions was undeniable. They were the most glamorous facet of Brunswick's growth, the most easily grasped component of Ted's dreams.

"Of course, that phrase, 'The General Motors of Sports' is what people grabbed on to," said a former board member. "The recreational acquisitions made good copy for the papers and caused a lot of excitement with stockholders. But Ted's dream was bigger than that, and when you look back, you can see how important some acquisitions in other areas were."

Especially important was the purchase of the A.S. Aloe Com-

pany in 1959, for it put Brunswick into the medical business in a big way. Like Brunswick, Aloe had a long, interesting history. Founded in 1858 by a Scotch-Irish immigrant named Albert S. Aloe, it began as an optical eyeglass shop in St. Louis. As it steadily expanded, its line grew to include cameras, photo equipment, and surgical and surveying implements. Louis Aloe took over after his father's death in 1893, and by the time of the 1903-04 St. Louis World's Fair he was selling such innovative products as microscopes on a time-payment basis, a method then unheard of in the medical business.

Louis Aloe was succeeded by

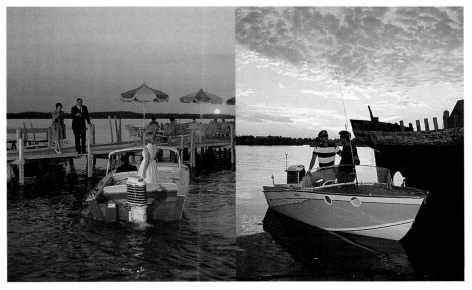

Scenes of Mercury in 1961, at the time it joined the Brunswick family. Mercury power helps boaters taste the good life as they *(upper left)* enjoy cocktails at dusk and *(upper right)* watch the sunset in a New England harbor. *(Below)* The breadth of the 1961 Mercury line is described in this magazine advertisement.

A. S. Aloe founded his company in St. Louis in 1858. When it was purchased by Brunswick in 1959, the A. S. Aloe Company distributed 30,000 medical items through its national catalogue.

Howard F. Baer who was a hunting and fishing acquaintance of Ted Bensinger's. When Ted expressed interest in buying Aloe, negotiations were friendly. The company, which by then distributed a startling 30,000 items through its national catalog, became part of Brunswick for $8.9 million.

With the acquisition of Aloe—along with the addition of the T. J. Noonan Company, Massey Surgical Inc., and Biological Re-

search—Brunswick had one of the nation's largest marketers of hospital and medical equipment. Though Brunswick's medical business began primarily as a distributorship, it wasn't long before Ted started looking for products which his company might not only market but manufacture as well. He found and acquired two such companies in 1961: the Sheridan Catheter and Instrument Corporation, and Roehr Products. Each company was owned by the sort of entrepreneur Ted so strongly admired.

Dave Sheridan, experimenting in a large red barn in Argyle, New York, spent the late 1940s looking for ways to make plastic tubing that would solve the many splicing, sterilization and inventory problems faced by hospitals and scientific laboratories. This tubing was mostly used as catheters, which were used in diagnostic procedures and in introducing and draining fluids from the body.

At the time, catheters were crudely constructed through a means of braiding, varnishing and baking. Sheridan worked for three years to invent a process by which catheters could be made continuously from clear plastic. His method perfected, he turned his barn into a factory and marketed his invention under the "Argyle" brand. His invention rendered old style catheters obsolete.

Equally innovative and successful was the owner of Roehr Products, Matt Roehr, a Polish refugee who had arrived in New York in 1940 with $50 in his pocket. A trained engineer, Roehr was determined to find a new way of making hypodermic needles. He bought a discarded grinder at a junkyard and transformed it into a machine capable of making 300 needles at a time. This method of mass production made disposable needles and syringes feasible. By the time Roehr Products was purchased by Brunswick, the company made 4.5 million needles every week, more than its closest competitor made in a month.

The medical industry was attractive to Ted for two principal reasons: growth potential and relative stability. "Health," he said,

"is as basic to our economy as are recreation, education, and defense. The need for better health care and hospital facilities is being emphasized more and more by local, state, and national governmental agencies as well as by innumerable private interests—thus assuring an expanding market for . . . products and services."

He was right. His medical acquisitions would eventually help the company withstand the financial troubles of the early 1960s and would become the basis for the later formation of Sherwood Medical Industries, the nation's second-largest enterprise in the manufacture, sales, and distribution of medical and laboratory supplies.

Working in a red barn in New York, Dave Sheridan perfected a new way of making catheters, rendering old methods obsolete.

Argyle catheters and Monoject disposable needles and syringes were products that made Sherwood Medical Industries a health care leader in the 1970's.

Of all the acquisitions Ted Bensinger would make, none would prove more important than that of the Kiekhaefer Corporation, the manufacturer of Mercury outboard motors.

Like many successful companies, the Kiekhaefer Corporation was a manifestation of one man's dreams and energy. His name was Elmer Carl Kiekhaefer, and he was a tough, strong-willed individualist descended from a family that had farmed Wisconsin land since the 1840s.

As a boy, he preferred tinkering with machinery to plowing, and attended the Milwaukee School of Engineering. In 1939, while working as chief engineer at Milwaukee's Stearns Magnetic Company, he bought a dying outboard motor company near his family's farm in Cedarburg, Wisconsin. With a small crew, he rebuilt the motors left behind by the previous owners. He sold them, and new orders started coming in.

He introduced the Mercury name at the New York Boat Show in the winter of 1939, affixed to motors of both single-cylinder and 2-cylinder alternate-firing designs. These motors incorporated a number of innovative engineering features that were later adopted by the entire outboard industry.

During World War II, when production of outboard motors was halted, Kiekhaefer set out to produce a portable saw for the Army.

E. C. Kiekhaefer, shown here in 1939 overseeing production of his first line of outboard motors, was an engineering genius who helped transform the marine power industry.

It was no simple task. For nearly 20 years, army engineers had tried to develop a portable power saw to replace the heavy, cumbersome models then in use. But in just two months, Kiekhaefer had completed a new machine, and in a test, the saw powered by the Mercury engine cut through a 24-inch green log in 17 seconds, as opposed to 52 seconds for its nearest competitor.

Mercury's design, a 2-cylinder-inline, alternate-firing, air-cooled powerhead of 15-cubic-inch displacement, was accepted by the Army. During the war, the company became a mass producer of such engines, later adding a model with 20-cubic-inch displacement that was rated at 12-horsepower.

At the war's end, Kiekhaefer anticipated an increased demand for larger and more powerful outboard motors. He was bent on expansion, though wartime restrictions on new construction remained in effect. Early in 1946, the newly-formed Association of Commerce of Fond du Lac induced Kiekhaefer to purchase 30 acres of the new industrial park on the southwest side of town. Included in that purchase was a two story barn still filled with 90 tons of hay. One of the handsomest barns in Wisconsin—300 feet long and 50 feet wide—it soon housed 130 Kiekhaefer employees.

The company's expansion perfectly coincided with the growth of the marine industry. Before the war, an outboard motor was mainly

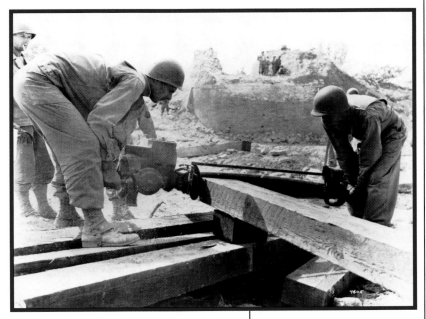

Using an engine of Kiekhaefer design, this portable saw amazed the U.S. Army by cutting through this block of wood in 17 seconds. Its nearest competitor took nearly a minute to do the job.

a device to get a fisherman to where the big ones were biting. A six-horsepower motor was regarded as big. But times were changing. With more money and more leisure time, tens of thousands of families were discovering boating. That required bigger boats and larger motors. Water skiing, once deemed a pastime for daredevils, became an important sport, and one that required even greater horsepower.

In 1947 Kiekhaefer introduced the Mercury 10-horsepower Lightning and then moved into higher-powered engines—such as the 40-horsepower, 4-cylinder in-line Thunderbolt, the 6-cylinder Mark 75, and others. As the market expanded, so did the company. It built a parts and ser-

This selection of Mercury motors through the years contains a number of technical innovations that later became standard for the entire marine power industry.

1940	Anti-friction needle bearings on wrist pins
1946	Anti-friction ball and roller bearings throughout
1947	One-piece die-cast aluminum two-cylinder blocks
1949	90-degree consecutive-firing 4-cylinder engines
1949	Four in-line design
1950	Forged aluminum clamp backups
1951	Transom through-bolt provisions in clamp brackets
1952	Impact-absorbing rubber clutch in propeller hub
1952	Automatic tilt-lock for reverse operation
1953	Toothed flexible belt utilized as magneto drive
1953	Production models rated over one hp per cubic inch
1954	12-volt alternator-type direct-drive generator
1954	Key-switch operation of electric starter
1954	Sealed, quick-disconnect remote wiring harness
1955	Sound-absorbent liners for engine covers
1955	1-piece die-cast aluminum 4-cylinder engine blocks
1957	Counter-rotating dual-motor installations
1957	12-volt automotive-type battery ignition system
1957	Single-lever remote throttle and shift control
1957	Propeller torque compensation built into lower unit
1957	Customer propeller choice to suit type of service
1958	Fixed jets replacing adjustable needle valves
1958	Hydraulic shock absorbers for impact protection
1958	Ignition tilt-switch co-acting with shock absorbers

vice division at Beaver Dam, Wisconsin; a boathouse, production plant, and research center at Oshkosh; and new production facilities in Cedarburg and Fond du Lac. From these locations, further innovations poured during the 1950s. The industry's first six-cylinder outboard, the 60-horsepower Mark 75, was unveiled at the 1957 inauguration of the company's Lake "ECK," Florida, proving ground (named in honor of the boss but more commonly referred to as Lake X.)

By 1960, the company had built a large plant at St. Cloud, Florida, for the manufacture of Mercury's line of Quicksilver accessories and aluminum pontoons made of high strength, corrosion resistant aluminum especially suited to salt water use. And that same year announced its first stern drive unit for inboard engines of over 100 horsepower at the Chicago National Boat Show. Named the MerCruiser, the unit offered larger boats the advantages of stern drive, utilizing engineering and safety features introduced on Mercury outboards over the years, coupled with the power and economy of large inboard marine engines.

As a privately held firm, Kiekhaefer Corporation did not publish annual financial statements. But from an initial investment of $53,500 in 1939, revenues had soared yearly. By 1960 industry estimates put the company's sales figure at nearly $50 million. The growth had been tremendous. Distribution was handled through a national network of 3,500 independent dealers. The firm had expanded to include plants in six Wisconsin and Florida cities, and three test bases.

But an economic downturn affecting the entire marine industry put Kiekhaefer's company in an increasingly difficult position. In 1961, in order to meet its debt obligations, it would have to go public or answer the calls from Ted Bensinger, eager to make the company part of Brunswick. While the thought of having his company owned by the public was abhorrent to Carl Kiekhaefer, neither was he enthusiastic about joining forces with Brunswick. "He just didn't hit it off with Ted," recalled a Mercury executive.

Kiekhaefer was one of a kind. He owned motorcycles—a 600 BMW, a Suzuki, and several Hondas. He owned cars—a

Lamborghini that he drove from New York to Philadelphia before discovering its fifth gear ("I thought it was revvin' a little high"), a Lincoln, a Cadillac, an Oldsmobile, a Buick, and others. In six years of racing stock and sports cars he excelled, taking three consecutive National Stock Car Championships. His affinity for speed and performance found an outlet too in his company's heavy participation in powerboat racing.

There were dozens of stories about him—racing Ferraris across dirt fields; burying defective cars with earthmovers; ordering Army tanks to patrol his game preserve near Lake X. . . . He had his admirers and some detractors.

"In every sense, Carl thought of the company as his personal property. He had built it and he was not eager to have anyone else poking around, interfering," said a former Brunswick board member. "I think what finally sold Carl was Ted's convincing him he would still run the entire show."

In the summer of 1961 Kiekhaefer sold his company, in exchange for $34 million worth of Brunswick common stock. He became a Brunswick Vice President and joined the Company's Board of Directors. He was, at the time, Brunswick's largest individual stockholder. His firm, he was told, would operate as an autonomous, wholly-owned subsidiary.

"I know Carl had second thoughts about the Brunswick

One can tell from Carl Kiekhaefer's expression that his relationship with Ted Bensinger was far from perfect.

This photo, taken in Mercury's Fond du Lac plant in the early 1960s, barely hints at the division's success.

deal," recalled Bob Anderegg, a former Mercury executive. "I remember the day we signed the papers. It was as if it hit him all of a sudden. The company he built was no longer going to be all his. He didn't want to leave his Chicago hotel room, but finally we went and signed the deal and drove back to Fond du Lac. To Carl, the whole scene was downright depressing."

Whatever Kiekhaefer's feeling at the moment, his company would play an increasingly important role in the company he so reluctantly joined. There was no way of knowing that then. The passage of time is the only way to keep score in the acquisition game. To casual observers, and some financial writers, it often seemed that Ted Bensinger's eyes, so to speak, were bigger

than Brunswick's stomach. In some cases they were proven correct. Charting the outcome of Ted's acquisitions is to witness a few corporate shipwrecks amid some spectacular successes.

But as 1961 ended, the future looked full of the prospect of continued prosperity for Brunswick. The number of Brunswick employees had swelled from 5,529 in 1958 to 16,400 in 1961, and the many new companies Ted had gathered into the fold were already making their presence and possibilities felt, cutting into bowling's share of the company's total sales. In 1958, bowling had accounted for more than 75 percent of the company's sales. By 1961, it accounted for less than 60 percent. Even so, the sport was still a huge piece of the corporate pie. But, it was about to crumble.

11 *The Bowling Crash*

The boom goes out of bowling and Ted Bensinger seeks outside help to get Brunswick out of financial trouble

Like a nightmare, it began slowly and without obvious pattern. A bowling center proprietor in Ohio was late with a payment for his Pinsetter . . . then another in New York . . . and another in Pennsylvania . . . and another in Ohio.

"No one wanted to believe what we were seeing," recalled Milt Rudo. "At first we just thought these were isolated incidents. Why worry? Bowling was still hot."

A market survey commissioned by Brunswick in 1961 reaffirmed that. The study, which looked at America and bowling on a county-by-county basis, concluded that the end of the bowling boom was nowhere in sight.

"Oh, that survey," said Rudo, rolling his eyes. "It reported that the market could easily absorb 300,000 lanes. This was at a time, remember, when there were only about 125,000 lanes in operation. So, there we were being told that we were just scratching the surface."

Few had expected the sales of Pinsetters and other bowling equipment to maintain their explosive pace forever. A gradual leveling off was anticipated, and even that looked years away. But by early 1962, there was a significant drop in the number of

As faddists and curiosity seekers drifted to other pursuits, many bowling centers had a disturbingly empty look.

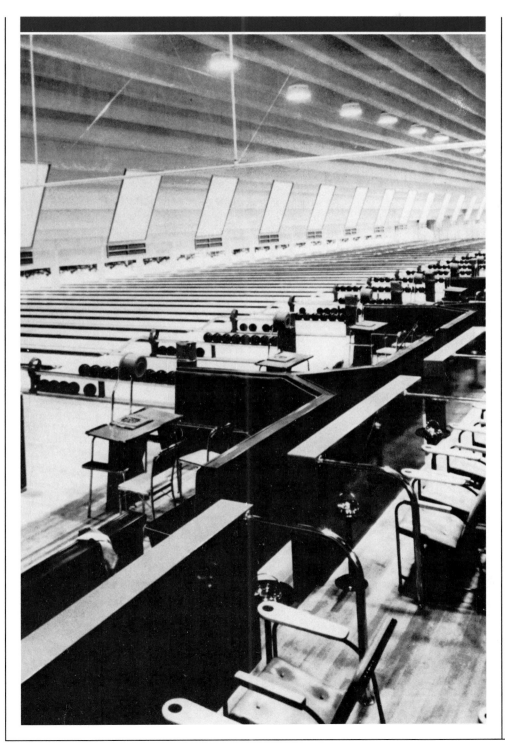

Where had all the bowlers gone? By 1963, the bowling boom was over.

bowlers as curiosity seekers and faddists drifted to other pursuits. This tremor was especially alarming to the hundreds of entrepreneurs who had spent and borrowed lavishly to build large, elaborate centers.

During the previous six years, while Brunswick raced with AMF to nail down new territories, the company had eagerly helped fi-

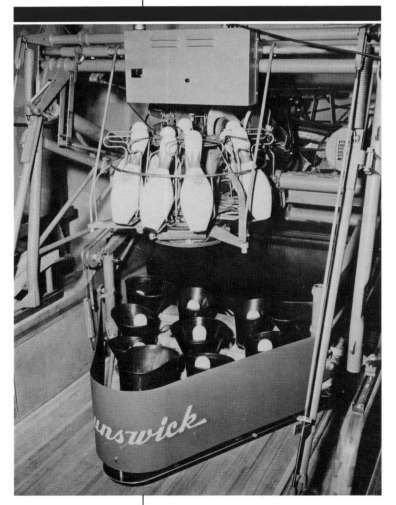

nance centers, often requiring as little as 10 percent down on its then $8,100 Pinsetters and 20-25 percent down on other equipment, with eight years to pay. The risk for proprietors and Brunswick looked rational in the face of blue-sky bowling statistics. But in the period of a few months in 1962, sales of Pinsetters dropped precipitously and hundreds of center owners, citing a fall off in players, insisted they could not meet their payments to Brunswick.

"To put it bluntly, the market had become saturated," said Rudo, who in 1962 was the head of Brunswick's bowling operations. "There had been a tremendous amount of overbuilding. A lot of people went into this business with blinders on, and those people got hurt."

Brunswick, too, began feeling the pain. The company had been borrowing huge amounts of money against future Pinsetter paydays. That was fine as long as Brunswick's customers continued to meet their financial obligations. But as the bowling boom began to go bust in 1962, Brunswick found itself saddled with $359 million in debts to a number of financial institutions. Nevertheless, with new centers closing and bad debts piling higher, the company held to the hope that bowling's downturn was a minor aberration and extended more credit in order to help proprietors.

As the company's financial hole got deeper, a number of bankers, executives and friends began suggesting to Ted that it would be in the company's best interest if he found someone to assist Brunswick in solving its financial difficulties.

"The suggestions were rather subtle at first," said Ed Stephan, a former member of the Board of Directors. "But it didn't take Ted long to realize that he didn't have the financial background to get the company through this crisis. I know that he was reluctant to believe things were ever as bad as the bankers implied. He always

felt bowling would make a quick rebound. But as sales and profits continued to dip, bankers began putting more and more pressure on Ted. Finally he gave in."

The facts were painfully clear. The value of Brunswick's stock dropped from $75 in 1961 to $13 in 1962, and profits plummeted 46 per cent to $24.3 million. By the summer of 1963, Ted arranged a meeting with Jack L. Hanigan, a 52-year-old executive and board member of the Dow Corning Corporation. Hanigan was highly

During the 1960s, billiards experienced a renaissance thanks to a film called "The Hustler," starring Paul Newman, Jackie Gleason, Piper Laurie, and George C. Scott. It re-introduced Americans to poolrooms around the country, and new facilities began to go up in suburban shopping centers and middle income neighborhoods. Many of these featured wall-to-wall carpeting, ersatz Tiffany lamps, and pastel tabletops. Most of them featured Brunswick tables. In 1966, some 3,000 new poolrooms opened, the majority called "family billiard centers." Though families sampled, they didn't stay. By 1970, this boom too was bust, and billiards would not again play a major role in Brunswick's operations.

MacGregor was the first choice of discriminating golfers such as young Jack Nicklaus.

regarded by the banking community, and his name was often mentioned when the topic of Brunswick's woes came up. Ted's problem was convincing him to come aboard.

"My initial reaction was not to join Brunswick," Hanigan recalled more than 20 years later, sitting near the swimming pool of his North Palm Beach, Florida home. "A mutual friend set up the meeting between myself and Ted. I liked him a lot, and his company's problems presented some interesting challenges."

The problems in the bowling business understandably overshadowed events taking place in Brunswick's other operations. Though revenues from these divi-

sions were not enough to offset the losses suffered by the bowling business, they did offer some encouraging signs.

In 1963, the School Equipment Division had acquired Burke, Inc., a Dallas-based furniture manufacturer, but nevertheless it experienced a downturn in sales and earnings. The three-year-old International Division realized a small operating profit before taxes; primarily concerned with the sale of bowling equipment in 42 foreign countries, this division was benefitting from the overseas sales of MacGregor golf clubs, balls, and bags.

Sales and earnings in the Defense Products Division showed an increase in 1963. A new plant was

Seemingly at home in this C-5 radome, a Defense Products employee puts a few finishing touches on his day's work.

brought into production in Lincoln, Nebraska to manufacture composite motor cases for rockets and missiles, and the division signed its first contract for the production of the Polaris A-3 second stage motor cases. It continued to be a leader in the field of high-performance aircraft radomes, receiving orders for McDonnell, Grumman, and Lockheed military aircraft.

The Health and Science Division, comprised of seven units—Aloe Medical, Aloe Scientific, Biological Research Inc., Brentwood, Roehr Chemicals Inc., Roehr Products Company Inc, and Sheridan Corporation—showed steady growth. It began selling into such new markets as nursing homes, and added a number of new products, such as diagnostic reagents. By 1963, plans were already underway to market this division's products on an international level.

The recreational businesses, of which the bowling operations were the largest part, was a beehive of various activities. The Bowling Division was marketing its new "A-2" Automatic Pinsetter and promoting bowling with such national programs as "Learn to Bowl" and "League Development."

The Marine Group, which included the Kiekhaefer-Mercury, Concorde (Owens) Yacht, and Zebco divisions, was in especially good shape. Zebco's sales and earnings trend was running seven per cent ahead of that for the overall fishing tackle industry.

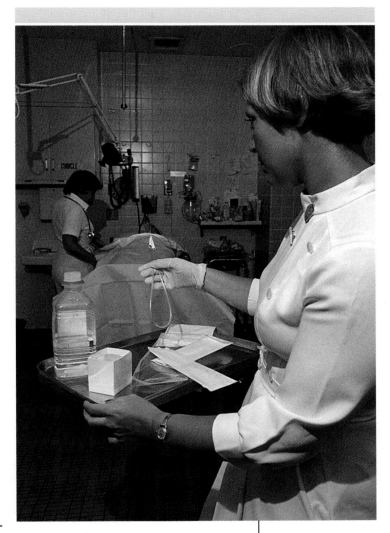

Owens had begun marketing a new line of 32-foot hulls and introduced two new cruisers—the 33-foot fiberglass Sport Fisherman and the 37-foot Express Cruiser. Also within the Recreation business unit, Brunswick's Sports Division—offering MacGregor sporting goods, Canadian Flyer ice

Almost any picture taken in a hospital would contain Sherwood products, such as these catheters.

The hit of 1963: In its first year of marketing, the MerCruiser stern drives became the best selling inboard/outdrive combination in the world.

skates, Union roller skates, Red Head outdoor clothing and life preserver boat cushions—appeared fit.

Kiekhaefer-Mercury registered the highest sales and earnings in its history in 1963. In its first full year of marketing, the new Mer-Cruiser stern drives became the largest selling inboard/outdrive combination in the world. Mer-Cruiser combinations of four-cycle inboard engines and outdrives were thriving; more than 165 boat builders were installing Mer-Cruisers as original equipment on their boats. Sales overseas, through International Mercury Outboards Ltd., maintained an excellent growth rate.

For those who continued to look at Brunswick simply as a bowling firm, the company in 1963 appeared badly bruised and battered.

But for those interested in looking behind the unfortunate situation in the bowling industry, Brunswick was also a company with its fingers in a lot of new and exciting fields. That was what Jack Hanigan was able to see with increasing clarity as he held meetings with Ted Bensinger. And eventually Hanigan made his decision. At a regular meeting of the Board of Directors on November 5, 1963, Hanigan was elected President of Brunswick.

"It is the Board's desire to elect a President who will devote all of his efforts to the effective day-to-day operations, while the Chairman would concentrate on planning for the orderly growth and development of the corporation," Ted announced at the time. "Brunswick is extremely fortunate in securing as outstanding an executive as Mr. Hanigan."

Ted retained his title of Chief Executive Officer and took over as Chairman of the Board. His brother Bob retired from that position, but remained a member of the board, eventually retiring in 1974. In giving up the reins of the company, Ted was making a decision that ended, but for the relatively short period when Hugh Collender ran the company, nearly 120 years of unbroken family leadership.

Ted was to remain a member of Brunswick's board of directors until 1976. At a formal dinner that year Ed Stephan, a Brunswick Board Member and attorney with Mayer, Brown and Platt, the company's legal counsel since the 1800s, spoke for many when he said, "Ted's style was always informal, flexible, and egalitarian. Some business reporter once wrote that the closest thing to the Brunswick executive offices was a men's locker room, but strangely this was a system in which familiarity did not breed contempt—but rather respect."

Not at all intimidated by the problems caused by the bowling crash, Jack Hanigan became President of Brunswick in 1963 and led the company out of its financial difficulties and boldly into new areas.

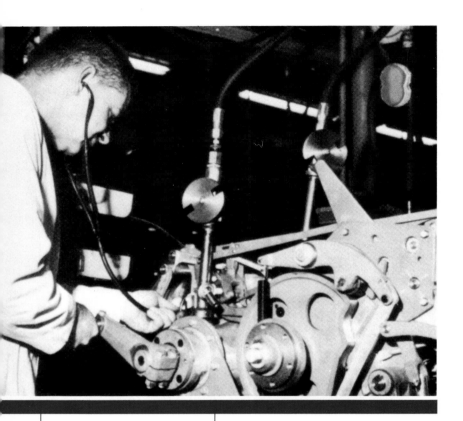

In the Fond du Lac factory, a Mercury employee carefully crafts another engine.

I think the whole situation in 1963 came as a terrible shock to Ted," observed Hanigan. The problems his company was experiencing stunned him. I liked him very much. He was a very imaginative guy. And though he was certainly hurt by what had happened, he was just desperate to get things fixed and he worked like hell with me to do it."

It wasn't easy.

"We had to get tough with our customers," said Hanigan. "I had some fear, at first, that we might not be able to collect the money we were owed. We had to make it clear, in no uncertain terms, that we were willing to take back our equipment if we weren't paid."

It fell to K. Brooks Abernathy to get that money. He had joined Brunswick in 1962 as Assistant Vice President and Credit Manager, after a successful career with General Electric and General Electric Credit Corporation.

"What helped tremendously was the viability of the Pinsetter," Abernathy recalled. "If it was lousy there would have been some defense for non-payment. But it was an excellent machine. We instituted very strong collection methods and the money began to come in. Certainly there were some who couldn't or wouldn't pay. For them we had only two alternatives: repossess the machines and try to resell them, or operate the centers ourselves.

A few years later executive Jim Urbanek reflected on Ted's contribution: "When the bowling crash came, it obscured much of what Ted had done. The same people who had cheered every move he made, blamed him for our problems. What they never realized was that without Ted's vision and energy the company would never have made it. Sure he bought a lot of companies and most of them helped see us through the hard times. He gave Hanigan a lot to work with."

Careful study convinced Hanigan of the latter idea's viability. He believed that professional management could save dozens of troubled bowling centers and offer Brunswick a fighting chance of getting its money back.

Milt Rudo was put in charge of the new Bowling Center Operations Division in 1964, and he organized teams to evaluate centers. More than 300 were assessed and by the end of 1965, the company had taken possession of 131.

"We had no idea how to run them, " said Rudo. "All Hanigan said was, 'Do one thing. Don't lose any money.'"

Turning around the bowling centers was but one part of Hanigan's plan to fix Brunswick. Of immediate, if not more complex, concern were the company's dire money matters.

In 1963, the company reported losses of $10 million. The following year it registered a modest $602,000 profit. In 1965, the board of directors set up a $76 million reserve to cover losses and bad debts. Since this loss after audit would have breached major covenants in company's loan agreements, new loan agreements were signed the following spring. The company also that year received a tax refund of $18 million from the IRS.

In 1966, as Hanigan took over as Chief Executive, the company paid off $66.1 million in debt and reported net earnings of $3.1 million.

That summer Hanigan had displayed guarded optimism when he told a group at Harvard, "I am confident that our financial crisis is behind us." But like everyone in the company, he knew there was much work ahead.

The start of something big: Colt Lanes became one of the first properties acquired by the Brunswick Bowling Center Operations Division in 1965.

12 A Clear Assignment

"Steering" the company was Jack Hanigan's daunting mission

Jack Hanigan

The mid-1960s present a dizzying number of corporate alterations—"a change every day," one executive recalled—as Jack Hanigan started to build on the foundation Ted Bensinger had provided him and change the face of Brunswick.

"Hanigan had a clear assignment," said former executive Jack Meyerhoff, "It was steer the company, and toward that end he exhibited total pragmatism."

Divisions were born and divisions vanished. Realignments were frequent, swift and sometimes confusing. American business in the 1960s was characterized by a trend toward building conglomerates. The prevailing wisdom, at Brunswick and elsewhere, was that good managers could run any business, no matter how far

afield it seemed—or, indeed,was—from a company's core business.

Ted Bensinger had initiated the conglomerate dream with his aggressive buying strategy—his vision of building "the General Motors of Sports." Hanigan too wished to transform Brunswick into a conglomerate, though his emphasis was not much on recreation—the bowling bust having been for him a painful lesson in the cyclicality of such businesses—but rather on new technologies.

One of his most significant actions was the 1965 formation of a Technical and New Business Division. It consisted of a research team; product development and engineering organizations; and a new products division which became deeply involved in the production and marketing of Brunsmet, a metal fiber product line. Developed at a cost of $10-million, Brunsmet had many applications. It could be woven together with carpet fiber to provide anti-static properties (and would lead to the 1974 purchase of Ozite, a Chicago-based maker of indoor-outdoor carpet for $14-million); made into an abradable seals for the new generation of high thrust engines; or used for sophisticated performance filtration media in aerospace and industry.

It was apparent to Hanigan that such new technologies had applications for the defense industry and in

Fostered by Hanigan and developed at a cost of $10 million, the company's new metal fiber would prove to have many applications. Among the first was as an addition to carpet fibers to provide anti-static properties.

Technical, medical, marine power, and recreation—the businesses of Brunswick are depicted in dramatic sculptural style for the cover of an Annual Report.

Sherwood's Argyle® medical tubes, catheters and other tubular products – a leading choice of doctors and hospitals

1967 the Defense Division and Technical and New Business Division were incorporated into a Technical Products Division.

The next year, another change occurred when Hanigan formed Sherwood Medical Industries, Inc., composed primarily of Aloe Medical, Roehr Chemicals, Inc., Roehr Products, Inc., Biological Research, Brentwood, Sheridan Corporation, and P.M. Steel Products—all companies purchased by Ted Bensinger.

The assets of Aloe Scientific Inc. were sold and at the same time the company discontinued calls on individuals by the Aloe sales force. Sherwood became a separate company—a wholly owned subsidiary—in 1968 when Brunswick sold a 15 percent stock interest to the public. Sherwood made and marketed more than 30 brand names, including industry leaders such as Monoject disposable needles, Argyle tubes and catheters, and Lancer laboratory products.

This represented an important strategic thrust. Hanigan was determined that the company should be distributing only products which it made, thereby providing greater controls and efficiency.

Nineteen sixty-eight also held a pleasant surprise: the Bowling Center Operations Division started turning a profit. It hadn't been easy. Winning the confidence of other center owners had been difficult. At first they were reluctant to believe the "we're all in this together" spirit Brunswick tried sincerely to foster. Times were tough. But the industry began to believe, as Brunswick became the point man in the effort to stabilize the bowling industry. Commissioning studies, reports and surveys, Brunswick shared all of its research with the owners and the media.

Also making Hanigan's corporate life easier during the mid-1960s was the spectacular growth of Mercury.

In 1964, when Mercury celebrated its 25th anniversary, ground was broken on the first phase of a multi-million dollar expansion of the facilities in Fond du Lac, adding nearly 500,000 square feet. The following year the division experienced tremendous growth in Canada as the international and U.S. market responded enthusiastically to the company's economical 60-horsepower MerCruiser. In 1966 Mercury introduced the 100-horsepower Merc 1000SS, the most powerful outboard ever built, and followed that with an even more powerful 125-horsepower engine; the six-in-line engine called the "Tower of Power." These important innovations coincided with another second major phase of Mercury's $9-million expansion program—the construction of an additional 370,000 feet of plant area in Fond du Lac.

The new buildings included an engineering center, a heat treating plant, and a giant facility consolidating assembly, paint and test operation. Led by the indomitable Kiekhaefer, Mercury thrived, its sales figures quadrupling between 1961 and 1969, when they topped $135-million.

"Many of Carl's contribution have been buried by the years," said former Mercury executive Bob Anderegg. "He was a genius with machinery, and the growth of Mercury, especially during the 1960s, was the result of his determination and desire for constant improvement in products, and his ability to give real life to his dreams.

When Carl had an idea, it usually changed the face of the industry."

There is no way to overestimate Kiekhaefer's success with Mercury or his influence on the marine power industry. But as Mercury grew to become a larger part of Brunswick, so did its day-to-day operations attract greater attention from corporate headquarters. This was only natural: as large investments are made, so are those investments more closely watched. Inevitably, this put a strain on the

The hugely successful MerCruiser is shown in close-up and moving along the assembly line in Fond du Lac.

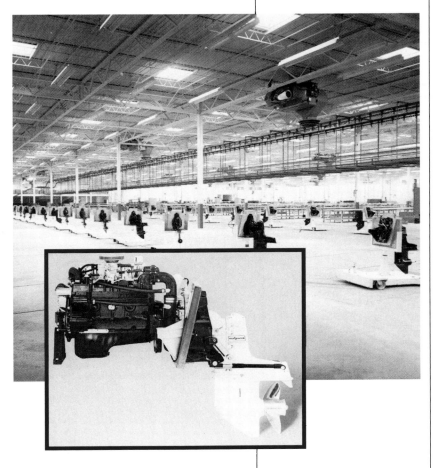

relationship with the fiercely independent Kiekhaefer.

"Carl thought he could run the whole operation from his desk," recalled Anderegg. "But the growth was so dramatic, I'm sure he saw the handwriting on the wall." One way or another he knew he would have to give up hands-on control of the company. It was no longer a one-man show. And so, in 1969, Brooks Abernathy, who had most recently been head of the company's international businesses, was named to replace Kiekhaefer as President of Mercury.

Late in 1970, Newsweek Magazine sent a reporter to the company's headquarters on Washington Street in Chicago. What he found was a company vastly different from what it had been a decade before. The reporter met

with Hanigan, who had just returned from a trip to Japan for the opening of a sports complex that included bowling, billiards, and indoor golf; part of a joint venture between Brunswick and Mitsui called Nippon Brunswick which was formed in 1960.

The two men talked for an hour. Hanigan spoke deliberately when discussing some of the changes that had taken place in recent years: the growth of Sherwood Medical Industries and the expansion of Brunswick's technical businesses; the closing of the company's bowling centers in Australia in 1966, and the closing of a factory and more centers in Italy; the selling of Red Head in 1968; the sale of the school furniture line in 1969 and the later sales of Owens Yachts and Larson Boat Works.

Hanigan was understandably more animated when talking about Brunswick's sales in 1969: $450-million, which topped the company's previous record, 1961's $422-million.

"This is a whole new company," Hanigan told the reporter. "Brunswick is a company that just happened in the last 15 years."

Indeed. In 1955, Brunswick had been a relatively small bowling and billiard company struggling to get an automatic pinsetter to market. By 1970, through boom and bust, it had become less recognizable as a bowling company. With its new emphasis on the medical and technical fields just starting to be felt and the marine power business prospering,

Brunswick's expertise at making sophisticated radomes resulted in increasingly larger contracts.

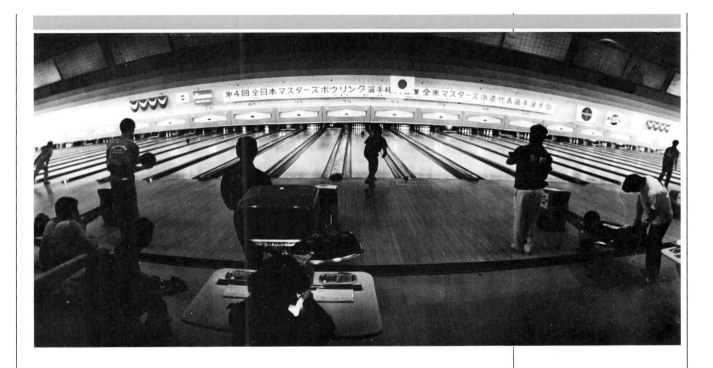

第4回全日本マスターズボウリング選手権　全米マスターズ派遣代表選手選考会

Brunswick was presenting a picture of a growing and stable conglomerate that the financial community was finding very attractive.

Under Abernathy's presidency, Mercury was thriving: sales increased from $150.4-million in 1970 to $267.9-million by 1972. But in 1973, an Arab oil embargo and the ensuing energy crisis threatened future sales. Instead of becoming edgy, the company quickly moved to position itself for inevitable recovery, revamping its motor line, and making dramatic engineering improvements and breaking ground for new manufacturing facilities in Stillwater, Oklahoma, for its increasingly successful stern-drive business.

The recession hit the entire company. In 1974 earnings dipped slightly, after eight consecutive years of increases. Reacting to this change in business climate, Hanigan and Abernathy, who had become President of Brunswick in 1972, began a reorganization of the company into four business groups—Medical, Technical, Marine Power and Recreation—with a number of divisions within each of them. It was their desire to grow each of these groups into equal parts of the corporation's revenues—a sturdy four-legged corporate stool—thereby allowing the entire business to better withstand the often dangerous valleys of the business cycle.

This vulnerability had just been

When bowling boomed in Japan, it wasn't unusual to see people stopping on their way to and from work to bowl a few lines.

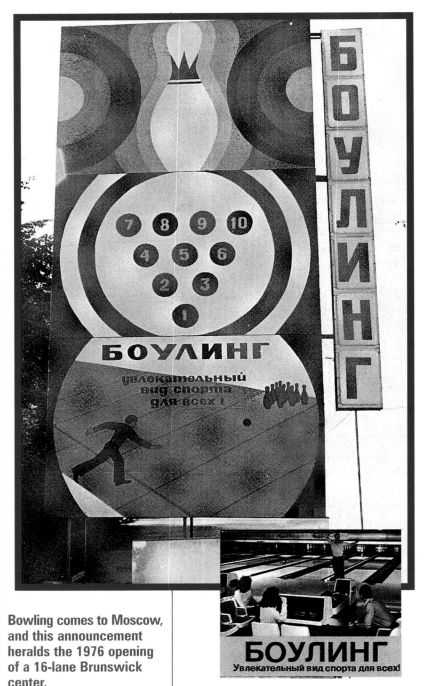

Bowling comes to Moscow, and this announcement heralds the 1976 opening of a 16-lane Brunswick center.

on vivid display in Japan, where bowling was playing out an interesting, if frighteningly familiar scenario. Though there were only about 500 bowling lanes in Japan during most of the 1960s, late in the decade bowling fever hit the country. People could be seen carrying bowling balls to work, often stopping for a few games in the morning and returning after work, sometimes bowling until midnight.

To meet this demand, centers began to rise around the country, centers with 50, 60 and more lanes. As a result of this surging activity, the lane population soared; and a few short years later, the number of lanes installed in Japan peaked at over 100,000.

And then, mirroring the sport's misadventures in the U.S., it all fell apart. Corporate net sales of bowling products to Nippon Brunswick plummeted from $64-million in 1973 to $1-million the following year.

The company's other international ventures were not experiencing such trauma. With Abernathy spearheading the international push, Mercury built its first European plant at Petit-Rechain, Belgium, and began producing outboard motors there in 1972.

What would prove a major growth strategy took place that same year with the formation of a joint venture with the Japanese firm Yamaha. This joint venture, called Sanshin and started by Abernathy and Jack Reichert, was an agreement to produce and market a new line of outboards. Sanshin would design and manufacture a line of outboards for Yamaha under the Yamaha brand, and for Brunswick under the name Mariner. Originally, they were basically similar engines.

"I had the opportunity to select the name Mariner," recalled Reichert. "We wanted something that would have an image different than that of the high-performance image of Mercury and the idea of the Ancient Mariner—of reliability and durability—seemed to fit."

Reichert had become President of Mercury in 1972, when Abernathy left that position to become Brunswick President. The announcement was made at the annual shareholders meeting and it was, Reichert recalled, "a huge shock."

A native of West Allis, Reichert had joined Brunswick in 1957, as a 26-year-old. At Brunswick he worked in the bowling division for 14 years, was instrumental in the formation of the company's retail bowling business and eventually rose to Vice President for Marketing. In 1971, he arrived in Fond du Lac for a similar position with Mercury. In less than a year he was named President.

"Why me?," said Reichert. "I think that after Carl [Kiekhaefer] left and after Brooks [Abernathy] had been in control for three years, there was within Brunswick a sense that the job should continue to be held by a Brunswick, rather than Mercury person—to some one who was part of, who understood, the Brunswick culture.

Jack F. Reichert

13 *Target For Takeover*

An orchestrated growth attracts unwanted attention

K. Brooks Abernathy was determined that Brunswick continue to concentrate on new technologies, such as those with applications in the medical industry.

"An Environment For Results." That's what Brooks Abernathy was determined to create when he became Chairman and CEO of Brunswick in 1976, following Hanigan's retirement.

The structure instituted two years earlier, when the company was organized into four business groups—Marine, Medical, Recreation and Technical—was completed by 1976 and Abernathy deemed that alternation essential "to accommodate the growth ahead." The next year Abernathy brought Jack Reichert from Fond du Lac to become Brunswick's President and Chief Operating Officer.

"It was difficult to leave," Reichert said. "Even though I had gone through a difficult strike in 1975, my feelings for the people of Mercury were very strong. Furthermore, I had gotten to know the marine business and really enjoyed it."

During Reichert's Mercury presidency, sales nearly doubled, from $168-million to $300-million; and he took great pride in establishing a new stern-drive facility in Stillwater, Oklahoma.His greatest accomplishment he felt was more personal.

"I think that my helping to bring

Skilled hands recheck the tolerance of Brunswick's Systems 2000 bowling lane – an advanced synthetic laminated composite designed to replace traditional wooden lanes.

In addition to its world-wide leadership in the leisure time field, by 1976 Brunswick products occupied important positions in health care, defense, fluid mechanics and aerospace.

The Defense Division, part of Brunswick's Technical Group, perfected the process of manufacturing filament-wound reinforced fiberglass for the U.S. army's Viper program and other defense projects.

Carl Kiekhaefer back into the company was the best thing I did," he said. "By doing that Mercury and Brunswick were finally able to come together."

It was hard to leave Mercury, but Abernathy was persuasive.

"He said that if I didn't take the job, he was going to go outside the company and look for some one else," Reichert recalled. "At that time I thought it was essential that the line of succession should stay within the company. I said 'Yes'."

Growth appeared certain. The company was rebounding nicely from the economic recession of 1975, which had been compounded by the seven-week strike at Mercury. In 1977 the company, with more than 25,000 employees, topped $1-billion in sales for the first time.

"Brooks was determined to conserve the gains the company had made. They had been very hard won," said former executive Jim Urbanek. "He wanted to build slowly and conservatively. He wanted the company's progress to be formalized, well-orchestrated, planned to the smallest details. With the bottom line always in mind, he never jumped feet first."

Sherwood was playing an increasingly important role, experiencing steady internal growth, supplemented by gradual expansion. It was apparent that the operation's manufactured items were more profitable than others, which it merely distributed. As a result, in 1978 the Aloe medical resale and distribution business was discontinued, and total focus was given to the manufacture of disposable medical items.

The Technical Group, which Abernathy deemed the company's "fastest growing area" in the mid-1970s, included the Defense and Technetics Divisions, which produced a diversified and complicated collection of high tech products that had a variety of uses in many fields. The Defense Division turned out such items as the boom arm for the Viking Mars Lander; radomes for military aircraft; composite motor cases for missiles and rockets; and a variety of transportable shelters. Technetics began in the filtration and abradable seal businesses, and with the 1977 acquisition of Circle Seal of Anaheim, California, its business expanded into valves and seals, regulators and controls used in a number of industries.

Abernathy moved Brunswick into such new fields as energy and transportation the following year, with the purchase of the Vapor Corporation. At $92 -million, it was the largest acquisition thus far in the company's history.

Founded in 1904 by Egbert H. Gold as the Chicago Car Heating & Lighting Company, it was one of the country's leading manufacturers of heating systems for railway cars. It had expanded into door opening systems, fare collection boxes, climate control systems, relays, speed indicators, steam generators and many other products. Vapor's sales at the time exceeded those of either the Defense or Technetics Divisions, and it was designated a separate division within the Technical Group.

While that group expanded, the Recreation Group became leaner and, more importantly, the compa-

ny's cash cow. During the late 1970's, Abernathy sold off the marginally profitable MacGregor golf club, basketball and baseball products, plus the skiing and archery businesses of the company. These were among the businesses Ted Bensinger had purchased in his desire to make Brunswick "the General Motors of Sports." But they were deemed, by Abernathy, as they had been by Hanigan, too cyclical to remain part of the company.

But the rest of the Recreation Group was remarkably vital. During

With the purchase of the Vapor Corporation, a firm originally known as the Chicago Car Heating & Lighting Company (picture at left), Brunswick was into the energy business with Vapor's line of valves, shown below.

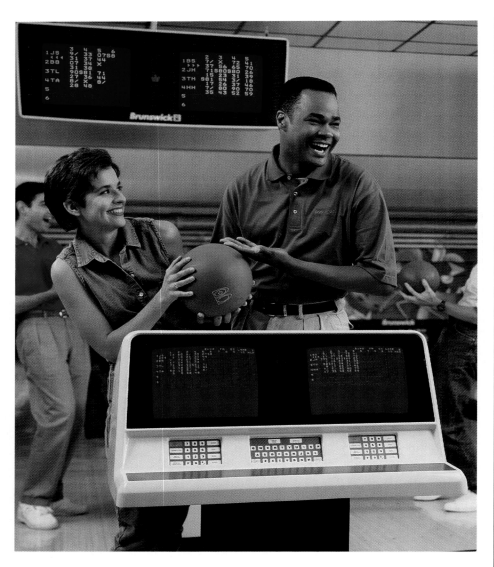

Pioneering in the development of automatic scoring, Brunswick led bowling into the electronic age during the final quarter of the 20th Century.

this period the Brunswick Recreation Centers Division operated 250 bowling centers worldwide and provided welcome cash flow that was used to fund the technical acquisitions. The Brunswick Division continued to produce bowling and billiard equipment at a profit, introducing such innovations as the Systems 2000 laminated bowling surface to replace older wooden lanes and, in 1967, the first automatic scoring systems, which were based on patents licensed from Eugene Reynolds, who is generally acknowledged to be the inventor of the automatic scorer.

Zebco, a separate division within the Recreation Group, grew steadily in sales and earnings during this period. During the mid-1970s it boosted its market share to more than 60 percent of all spincast reels purchased in the United States. With the number of avid anglers increasing rapidly, the company soon expanded into spinning reels — another hit.

The Marine Power Group had proven adept at dealing with the precarious economy. MerCruiser had become the group's fastest growing division, soaring to record sales. In 1975, it introduced an aluminum block engine, V-8 sterndrive power, and also the first company-made 4-cylinder diecast engine designed specifically for stern-drive use.

The Mercury Outboard Division, continuing to emphasize fuel economy, polishing its already glittering image as the dominant maker of high performance engines by continuing its technological dominance. The Mariner Division, which introduced its outboards in North America in 1976, expanded by adding dealers and distributors to its network as consumer acceptance of the Mariner line grew. In addition, Quicksilver parts and accessories business thrived, and became the most profitable of Mercury's operations.

Even as it was affected by two mid-1970's oil embargoes and the resultant recessions, the Marine Power Group set sales records throughout the decade. In 1980, another embargo all but paralyzed the U..S. economy. That, combined with a proposed governmental ban

on weekend boating—meant to ease the oil shortage but which was never implemented—significantly reduced domestic sales. A number of cost-cutting programs were initiated, including the closing of four feeder plants in Oshkosh and Cedarburg, Wisconsin, and the opening of a component parts plant in Juarez, Mexico. The results were markedly positive: a turnaround in operating earnings in 1981 amounting to an upswing of more than $50 million in sales over the previous year. In spite of the performance, the stock price did not reflect the improvement.

The brighter economic outlook made 1981 a record year for Brunswick. Since 1970, company sales had grown an impressive 125 percent. International sales—fueled

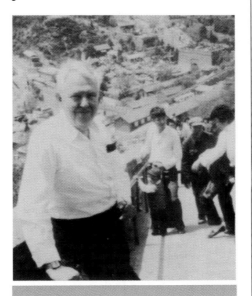

Brooks Abernathy, shown here at the Great Wall during a visit to China, would be a driving force behind Brunswick's international expansion.

by Abernathy's multinational vision—increased 460 percent in the decade, accounting for more than 24 per cent of the company's total revenue. Earnings for 1981 were a record $66-million.

The company's new and prosperous look began to attract unwanted investor interest. This was an era of merger mania—supported by LBOs [Leveraged Buy Outs] and so-called Junk Bonds. It was a time of takeover frenzy and many Wall Street analysts thought Brunswick vulnerable for a takeover attempt. "When you looked at the stock price of $18-a-share in relation to the book value of $25," said one New York analyst, "you could see that the company's pieces were worth more than the whole pie. And that's the kind of thing that makes for a pretty takeover picture."

January 24, 1982. Abernathy was sitting in the living room of his suburban Chicago home, watching the end of the Super Bowl game between the Cincinnati Bengals and the San Francisco 49ers, when the telephone rang. On the other end was Joseph Albrandi, president and CEO of Whittaker Corporation, a Los Angeles-based conglomerate. In a brusque manner he announced to Abernathy that Whittaker would attempt to buy Brunswick.

A messenger arrived at Abernathy's home within the hour, carrying the details of Whittaker's deal. It was offering $26.50 a share for 10.4 million of the outstanding Brunswick shares, plus an offer to buy $30-million in convertible debentures, the equivalent of what would later be known as junk bonds. If successful Whittaker would control 49 per cent of Brunswick's voting stock.

"I was angry," Abernathy recalled, "I was surprised by the aggressive nature of the offer. It was very sudden. And it was not a good offer."

Newspaper headlines boldly chronicled the battle for survival that Brunswick successfully waged against the takeover minded Whittaker Corporation.

go Sun-Times, Thursday, February 25, 1982   business

Whittaker extends offer to buy Brunswick shares

hittaker Corp. said it is extending its to buy Brunswick Corp.'s securities to ch 12 from its original date of Feb. 26. nwhile, Whittaker said a federal court is expected to rule Thursday on its on to have Brunswick's proposed sale of herwood Medical unit to American Home Products declared illegal. Brunswick, meanwhile, said it is confident it will be able to move forward with the sale. Separately, several analysts say that Brunwick "will lose its attractiveness" if it sells Sherwood, the "fastest- growing, highest profit" sector of Brunswick's business.

By the following morning, board members and executives were gathered at corporate headquarters in Skokie. They did not take kindly to the offer and, at a special meeting three days after Super Bowl Sunday, the company turned down Whittaker's offer and decided to fight the takeover.

It would be a bloody battle.

It was obvious what Whittaker wanted most from Brunswick: Sherwood. Whittaker was mainly a distributor of medical products, mostly in the Middle East. The purchase of Brunswick would give it the broad-based, international medical manufacturing business that would make it competitive with other firms in the industry.

The nature of the proposed package indicated that Whittaker would be forced to sell almost all of the rest of Brunswick in order to reduce its debt obligations. Brunswick brought a lawsuit against Whittaker on the grounds of anti-trust violations and the unfairness of its proposed transactions.

That takeover scenario proposal was unacceptable to Brunswick. A "white knight," a friendly company that might purchase a controlling interest in Brunswick and thus thwart Whittaker, could not be found. "A lot of companies were interested in buying parts of us," recalled board member Ian MacGregor. "But what most seemed to want was the medical business."

In the end a deal was struck with American Home Products to

The products and people of Sherwood, here represented by a lab technician and a colorful panorama of its needles and syringes, began to attract the interest of some take-over minded companies.

acquire Sherwood, a wholly owned subsidiary of Brunswick, in a stock swap agreement. In essence, American Home Products offered Brunswick shareholders $30 per share, up to a maximum of 14.2 million of the 26 million shares outstanding, a pro rata tender for 54 percent of the shares outstanding. American Home Products then exchanged this block to Brunswick for all the shares of Sherwood.

"The move seemed highly beneficial to both Brunswick and American Home, a big manufacturer of drugs and household items," reported the New York Times during the transaction. "Assuming the deal went through, not only would it deprive Whittaker, a company with interests in box cars, chemicals, and

health care, of Brunswick's key Sherwood operation, but also would have sharply reduced outstanding shares. This, in turn, would increase earnings per share on Brunswick's remaining operations."

Whittaker sued Brunswick in Federal Court claiming the defense by selling the medical business was unlawful. The court ruled in Brunswick's favor. On March 8, Whittaker withdrew its offer. The following day Sherwood was disposed of for 14.2 million shares of Brunswick stock that American Home Products had received through its tender offer. The deal amounted to $425 million, all of which went to shareholders.

The transaction, however, did not sit well with some. More than one

Sherwood employee felt "like a child who had just been abandoned by its parents." Other critics, many of them in the media, denounced the deal as "selling the crown jewels" and questioned the performance of the board during the takeover.

"It took a lot of strength to make the decision we did," remembered Reichert, who had been the only person to be called as a witness and to testify at the trial. "The Board knew that we'd be ripped to pieces. Few outsiders really understood all the complexities of what really happened. This was one of the most crucial periods in the company's history. Can you remember how many companies were being gobbled up and broken apart during the takeover frenzy of the 1980s? We survived thanks to a board that acted with great courage."

Later in March, Brunswick announced that it had to significantly reduce its corporate staff. Though the company provided additional special benefits for departing employees, it was not pleasant scene in Skokie, even for some of those who survived.

"It was a terribly difficult time," said one who remained with the company. "There was a sense of uncertainty. Were we going to get pink slips in our pay envelopes?"

In what the *Chicago Tribune* characterized as a "surprise move," Abernathy announced at the annual stockholders meeting in April, 1982, that he would retire one year earlier than scheduled and that Reichert would take over as Chief Executive Officer of Brunswick.

14 *The Reichert Era Starts*

Talking values, people and quality, Jack Reichert becomes the boss

Abradable seals made by the Technetics Division were an essential component of many jet engines.

After he became chief executive officer of Brunswick, Jack Reichert was offered a lot of advice, most of it unsolicited.

"Get rid of Mercury and all the other recreational businesses," he was told. "Concentrate on the technical end of the company."

Reichert listened. But he didn't like what he heard and rejected the advice, "People were telling me that Sherwood had been our only good operation," Reichert said. "And that made me angry. I couldn't accept that opinion. Because of the trauma at the time—there's no doubt that Brunswick was an injured compa-

ny—many people lost sight of the fact that we were in good businesses, and had leadership positions in some of them."

He was determined. On many nights he sat up late making plans, writing down his goals and expectations for the company. Brunswick was solid, he believed, but it needed to change quickly and dramatically to overcome the effects of Whittaker's takeover attempt and the disposition of Sherwood.

It was Reichert's belief that by decentralizing the company he could reduce costs while improving efficiency and response time. He

"A lot of people don't understand numbers. But everyone understands values," said Jack Reichert, shortly after becoming Brunswick's Chief Executive Officer.

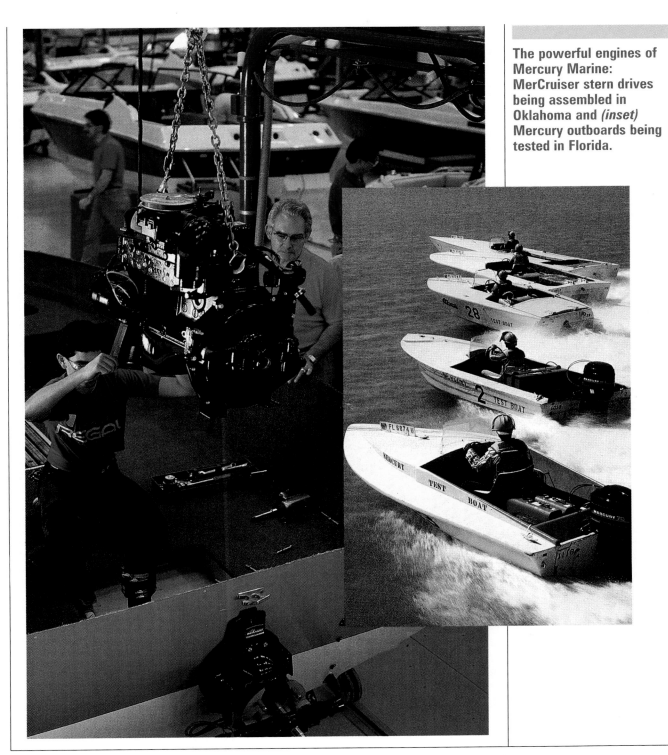

The powerful engines of Mercury Marine: MerCruiser stern drives being assembled in Oklahoma and *(inset)* Mercury outboards being tested in Florida.

was also determined to divest those businesses in which the company, for one reason or another, could not be in leadership positions; to retain and fix Brunswick businesses which need fixing; and to enhance the growth of existing businesses through acquisitions.

It was a straightforward strategy emphasizing Brunswick's leadership positions and built on a sturdy foundation of basic values. Reichert says he "agonized over identifying the company's values. At one point I came up with a list of 12 things and one of my executives said, 'C'mon Jack. Moses only had 10.' After about nine months I was finally satisfied."

This is what he wrote:

"Quality—we will either be the highest quality producer in every market we serve or we won't be in that business," he wrote on one of those late nights.

To that he added, "Customers— we are in business to serve customers at a profit. Singularly, customer satisfaction is the most important responsibility we have to assure long-term success of the company."

And this: "People—of paramount importance is our people—their personal dignity, their pride in what they do and the trust they have in management."

"A lot of people don't understand numbers," Reichert said. "But everyone understands values."

With those values guiding Reichert, the company began to change. Knowing that corporate change is never easy, Reichert's first move was to reject a $70,000 salary increase, feeling that "sacrifice must start at the top. He then began to restructure and streamline the company.

"The pyramid was too tall and too cumbersome," he said. "The levels of supervision had gotten so deep that it inhibited the sort of quick actions that were necessary."

Hanigan and Abernathy had

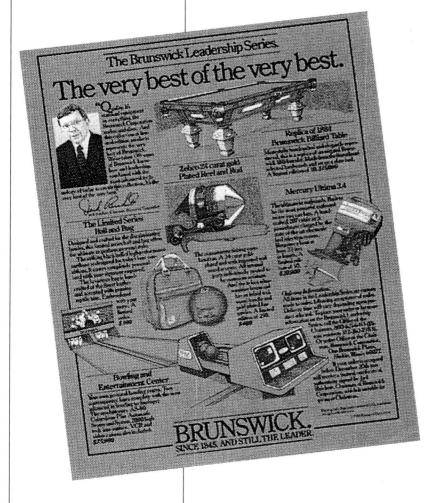

been devotees of strong central control and insisted that all important decisions be made in Skokie. At one point seven division presidents and two group executives were officed in Skokie. Reichert had been an exception; as President of Mercury in Fond du Lac, he was one of only two group vice presidents not physically tied to corporate headquarters.

"They were after me to move down here," he recalled. "I told Jack Hanigan in 1975 that I was only an hour away by air if I was ever needed. One day I was summoned to Skokie by Hanigan. 'Be in my office in an hour,' Hanigan said. I hopped on a plane and made it in 50 minutes. It turned out Jack was just testing to see if I could get there quickly. The issue of moving Mercury headquarters to Skokie was never brought up again."

That sort of experience fueled Reichert's desire for streamlining.

"Corporate entities do not create wealth," he said. "People who design, make, sell and service products do. As I saw it, our job at corporate was—and is—to reinvest and preserve wealth; to strategically plan for the future and have appropriate controls in place."

Reichert increased the capital spending authority of the division presidents tenfold, from $25,000 to $250,000, in order to give "a sense of ownership and entrepreneurship to the divisions. Under the old system too many people had to sign off on decisions. If something didn't work out—or if something did—a divi-

Brunswick's corporate headquarters from 1971 to 1993 were in Skokie, a suburb north of Chicago.

sion president could point to 10 people who had participated in and approved of the decision. There were 12 tiers separating a foreman on the assembly line from me. There were only six when I was finished."

Authority was delegated to the lowest levels in each division—"If you want to know how to do a job right," Reichert often said, "ask the person who is doing it"—with less interference from corporate staff. The positions of Chief Operating Officer and Group Executive were eliminated, immediately cutting two tiers of management directly from the top of the organization.

Reichert consolidated the company's eleven divisions into eight. Staff at corporate headquarters was reduced by more than half. Two of the company's three jet aircraft were sold. The executive dining room was closed. In the process, some $25-million in annual corporate overhead vanished almost overnight.

Less than two years after taking over, Reichert could see his plans having a positive effect.

And the speed with which the company could make decisions and get things done increased dramatically.

In the next few months, the company divested four businesses and set about to fix those operations that needed fixing. Billiards operations became part of the Brunswick Division whose staff was relocated from the corporate offices in Skokie across Lake Michigan to Muskegon, Michigan, the site of its manufacturing facilities. Also, the Technetics division was moved to DeLand, Florida. By having management working more closely with manufacturing personnel, Reichert rightly believed that operating costs could be reduced and more emphasis placed on the quality of goods being produced.

One costly example of his desire to sell only high-quality goods was the total recall of the Mark Ten bowling ball because it did not meet company standards.

"This is going to cost us at least $1 million," Reichert was told. "And what are we going to do with all the balls recalled?"

"I don't care if you make rosaries for elephants," Reichert had answered. "We were not going to sell a product that's won't satisfy customers. Yes, the cost was enormous for the time [it would eventually be $2.5 million]. But we had to keep the trust of our customers."

In less than two years after taking over as Brunswick's CEO—the title of Chairman was added in the fall of 1983 when Abernathy retired—Reichert could see his actions having a positive effect on the bottom line and on the company's employees.

He cared about both. He was a visible boss, frequently visiting the company's far-flung facilities and stopping often to chat with the people working there. It was important to him that the more than 19,000 company employees feel a part of the operation. He wanted their work to be a meaningful experience in which they could justifiably take pride.

"Jack wanted the employees to have dignity, feel pride in what they do and in the company they were working for," said William Niemann, Brunswick's Vice President-Law and Secretary, who ended his 26-year career with the company in 1985. "And, when the employees feel that way, as Jack points out, the numbers take care of themselves."

Reichert also believed that actions speak louder than words and as 1983 drew to a close, he realized another goal—to make all of the company's eligible employees shareholders in Brunswick.

"I always had the desire to make our employees capitalists and give them a sense of ownership in the company," he said.

Toward that end, Reichert insisted that every employee get the same amount of stock regardless of their level or salary. The stock program was accomplished with the aid of the U.S. government's PAYSOP program, which at the time allowed companies to receive a tax credit for the cost of the grant to employees. But at Reichert's request, the Board added a bonus, matching the contribution covered under PAYSOP with a contribution right out of earnings. (After the PAYSOP program was ended by the government, Brunswick was one of few companies that continued to make annual distributions of stock to its employees and by the end of 1994 had made such distributions for 12 consecutive years).

"It was our people who were responsible for our strong performance in 1983, and this was a very visible way to demonstrate how much we appreciated their efforts," Reichert said. "We also told them that, as long as the company's performance continued to grow, they would continue to benefit from the program."

Reichert also encouraged an increase in pension payouts to all pensioners. Historically, only former salaried employees receive such increases, but in 1984, the pension committee authorized inclusion of former hourly employees in the increased pension benefit.

With the revitalized commitment of its people and favorable economic conditions, Brunswick enjoyed record success. In 1983, company sales were $1.22 billion and its net earnings were $66 million. In 1984, things were better still: $1.47 billion in sales and $94.2 million in earnings.

Brunswick stock reached an all-time high early 1985. And Brunswick's employees shared in the gains.

Brunswick, on the fore-
front of technology, pro-
vided more than 400 parts
– filters, pressure vessels
and seals–for the Space
Shuttle Columbia.

The price of Brunswick stock hit another all-time high in 1985—a high that would be bettered in 1987, when the third two-for-one stock split in five and a half years would occur. One director, Pierre Rinfret, seemed to be speaking for the entire company when he said, "Companies need to have a value system they can believe in. Jack spent a lot of time spreading his message, sharing his goals and expectations. And people believed. He had more than just catchy phrases. He had the ability to make them realistic goals. And this company went into high gear trying to attain them."

15 Setting a new course

Purchasing the world's two largest boat companies successfully returns the company it its roots

In 1986 Jack Reichert walked into the office of Fred Florjancic, Jr., then Brunswick's Vice President-Finance.

"Fred," Reichert said, pausing for effect, "you've always told me that you could raise a billion dollars, right?"

"Well, yes, I said that," said Florjancic.

"Well, you'll have to find it," Reichert said, "because we're going to buy the two largest boat companies in the world and it's going to cost us somewhere in the neighborhood of $800-million."

Florjancic had heard rumblings of Reichert's bold plans.

"It had come to the point where the company had to make a decision about its future," Reichert recalled. "We were generating large amounts of cash, and after repurchasing some stock, we had to determine whether to diversify or to concentrate our resources in a given business area."

During three lengthy meetings with the board of directors, Reichert recommended a concentration strategy. Directors agreed with the strategy and the plan to purchase the two boat companies proceeded.

There was a phenomenon taking place in one part of the boating industry during the mid-1980s. It was clear to management and the people at Mercury that the industry was changing. Beginning in 1984, discussions at Mercury included what was called BMT, which meant Boat, (outboard) Motor, Trailer. The concept was being pioneered in the industry, of having manufacturers package these elements for the consumer rather than having the dealers do it."

The pioneering Bayliner *Capri* revolutionized the recreational boating industry, when it combined boats, motors and trailers into complete nautical packages.

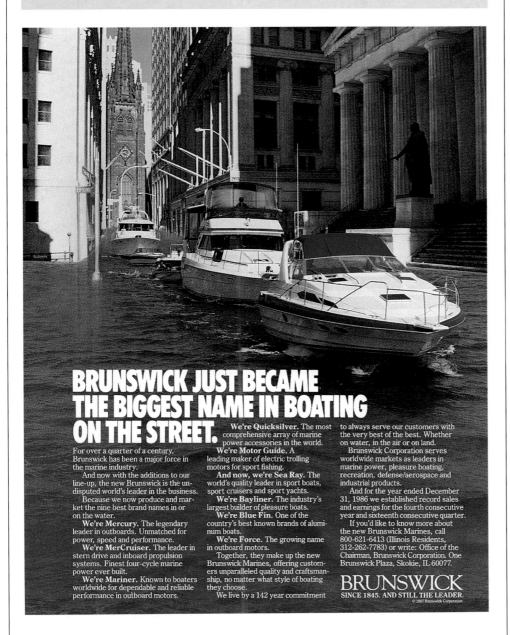

The addition of Bayliner and Sea Ray catapulted Brunswick into the role of undisputed boating leadership. That landmark event was announced in this unique advertisement; which pictured a Brunswick fleet cruising down the middle of Wall Street.

Reichert had asked [Mercury President] Dick Jordan to study the matter and present a plan. The two men met all day one Saturday, talking and debating at great length. Finally, after discussions with the board, a decision was made to go forward and make inquiries to the two biggest boat companies in the world.

If the company was going to get into the boat business, it would have to be with the best.

The two companies were Bayliner Marine Corporation and Sea Ray (Ray Industries). The acquisitions would eventually total $775-million. While there had been some consolidation in the marine industry during the 1980s, this transaction would be by far the largest. As Reichert would later tell the Wall Street Journal: "[The com-

bination is] just like when the carriage makers and the engine makers came together in the auto industry."

There is no historical evidence to pinpoint the birth of pleasure boating, beyond the fact that in the mid-1600s, Charles II introduced yachting into England. The first English yacht club was founded in 1775.

In the United States, pleasure boating began in the early 1800s and the first U.S. yacht club was organized in 1844 in New York City. Pleasure boating remained, for a century, a pastime of the elite. Not until after World War II did pleasure boating start its dramatic increase in popularity.

The number of boats grew from an estimated 2.4-million in 1947 to more than 8-million by the late 1960s. Much of that growth could be attributed to mass-production

Where it all began. From these humble beginnings on a vacant Seattle lot in 1955, Orin Edson took the first steps towards creating the world's best selling boat brand, Bayliner.

methods as well as the increased reliability of outboard motors.

Outboard motors became more dependable and less expensive. New inventions, such as electric starters, made it easier for people to operate boats. The amount of power produced by outboard motors also increased steadily, as did their reliability.

The use of fiberglass in boats in the 1960s as well as the introduction of stern drive power, and the use of expanded aluminum for fishing boats, made possible production-line techniques unthinkable under traditional boat-building. Innovations in styling and design made boats more appealing to a wider portion of an increasingly prosperous and leisure-minded public. Also, the increasing ease by which boats could be transported helped make boating accessible to those who previously had lived too far from navigable waters to make boating practical.

J. Orin Edson had just returned from the war in Korea and was searching for a career when two friends, boat-racing enthusiasts, asked Edson if he would sell a couple of used boats for them. The boats sold quickly. Edson soon leased a dusty vacant lot in Seattle and began to sell new and used pleasure craft under the name Advance Outboard Marine.

At the time, boats arrived at dealers far from ready to hit the waves. It was necessary for the dealers' employees to install deck hardware, lights, steering and often even windshields and seats. Then came the trailer and, lastly, the outboard engine. Edson—wisely, but with considerable effort—was able to become an authorized Mercury dealer and in short order became the biggest sellers of boats from Owens, Sea Ray, Reinell and others.

An entrepreneur to the core, Edson acquired the Bayliner line of boats from a company called Puget Plastics in nearby Arlington, Washington and in 1965 sold his first Bayliner boat in his Seattle dealership. The boats proved hugely successful and Edson began to expand his dealer network beyond the Northwest. In 1974 a new Bayliner production facility opened in Minnesota and three new models, called Buccaneer, were introduced. In 1980, another manufacturing facility opened in Georgia, giving Bayliner a presence in three important U.S. regions.

The following year, Bayliner revolutionized the industry by offering consumers a package of boat, outboard motor and trailer, instead of selling each separately. Though pleasure boats with stern-drive engines had been sold packaged since the 1960s, the rigging of virtually all outboard motors to boats was unheard of until Edson decided to, as he put it, "bet the company" on his novel marketing notion. He called it Total Value Packaging (TVP) and it began with the Capri, a popular 19-foot runabout. Previously any Capri buyer had a dizzying (and often frustrating) number of options; there were 36 different combinations of motors, styles and colors.

Bayliner, after much research into owner preferences, began to offer the Capri as a boat, motor, trailer pack-

This Mercury-powered *SRV 190* was one of the stars of Sea Ray's 1966 product line.

age. The company was therefore able not only to cut its own costs and establish lower prices for its dealers who placed larger orders, but most importantly, it was able to provide convenience for the consumer.

This packaging concept was so successful that the company was soon out of the dealership business altogether. In 1984 it purchased the physical assets of Chrysler Outboards. The money was available as a result of the company's stunning success; due primarily to the popularity of packaging and the Capri line, Bayliner's sales increased tenfold between 1982 and 1986.

C.N. Ray was an ambitious young man.

"I had the option of joining the family business that my grandfather had started, a prosperous sand and gravel business. But I wanted to do something else, make my own way," Ray recalled. "At the time new materials were making themselves apparent in many industries. Fiberglass and reinforced plastics were first being used for all sorts of things—golf cart bodies, caskets. I asked myself, 'Why not boats?'"

Ray rented a garage in the Detroit suburbs and started building boats.

"I thought I could play in the boat-building game," Ray said. "I thought of the business in automobile terms. I wanted to build the Cadillac of boats with Buick price tags. The idea, all along, was not to be the biggest. It was to be the best."

The first Sea Ray was unveiled at a

This sleek fiberglass cruiser was one of the many smartly styled models which catapulted Sea Ray to prominence in the 1970's.

135

Connie Ray *(left)* and Jack Reichert were all smiles, as they signed the agreements which made Sea Ray a part of the Brunswick family.

private party in 1960 at the Michigan Country Club in Orion, Michigan. The response was encouraging enough for Ray to decide that he would try to make and sell 150 boats a year.

But Ray knew that the market was vast. He had hired Harley Earle, the father of a friend and more importantly an interior design consultant at General Motors, to create sleek, finished interiors comparable to the quality and luxury of the automobiles of the time.

"I wanted something that would knock people's socks off," said Ray.

And that's what he got. In his first appearance at the Chicago Marine Trade Show in 1961, he received a spectacular response. In 1962, doors were opened at a new

plant in Oxford, Michigan. A second plant, in Phoenix, Arizona, opened in 1968; others followed, on Merritt Island on Florida's northeast coast; Knoxville, Tennessee; near Tellico Lake, Tennessee, and, in response to growing demand overseas, in Cork, Ireland.

Ray's philosophy was crystal clear.

"Our company is dedicated to building superior products: powerboats of high quality that perform well and offer excellent value for the price," he said. "No design, engineering or manufacturing challenge is too big, not any detail too small, for our team of outstanding engineers, who are continually looking for more ways to make a great product even better."

It was that sort of philosophy that produced intense customer loyalty and brand strength—the Sea Ray Line was generally regarded as boating's best. It had helped to build what one industry analyst called "a unique, almost unbelievably loyal" network of some 130 dealers who were intensely loyal to the company and its philosophy.

"Jack is the only person who could have bought these two companies. He had respect throughout the industry," recalled Dianne Yaconetti, who was instrumental in integrating the relationships between the boat companies and existing Brunswick operations. She

was homegrown, having joined the company as a 17-year-old in 1964 and spending most of her career working for Bill Niemann, Brunswick's Vice President-Law and Corporate Counsel. In 1985, when Niemann retired, Yaconetti became Corporate Secretary and a few years later a Vice President.

Indeed, Reichert had a long relationship with Ray, who had been the first boat builder Reichert invited to tour Mercury after he became president in 1972. He knew Edson only casually, though both men expressed admiration for one another.

"The only way to make this deal—or any deal—was to be straightforward and honest," Reichert said.

At a meeting with Edson,

Brunswick Azalea Lanes in Marietta, Georgia is one of the state of the art bowling centers which have keyed the rise of the BRC Division.

Reichert said, "What would your reaction be if I told you I'm also thinking of buying Sea Ray as well as Bayliner?"

"Wow," said Edson, "I never thought about it. But sure, we could live under the same tent. I really admire Connie and Sea Ray."

Reichert then went to a meeting with Ray at his hotel and told him about his intentions to acquire Bayliner and Sea Ray.

"Great," said Ray. "That would be the most spectacular thing in the world."

Though some skeptics believed the deal would never come off— "too many strong personalities involved," recalled one doubter— negotiations went smoothly and quietly until early November when it was announced that Brunswick would buy Bayliner Marine Corporation for $425-million. Then on December 1, the *Wall Street Journal* announced Brunswick's intention to also purchase Ray Industries for $350-million.

"It was not as hard a deal to make as many imagined," said Ray. "I had known Jack since his days at Mercury and knew him to be a man who could cut through the corporate b.s. He could make decisions. I was comfortable being with Jack."

The boating industry reacted swiftly, especially those at Outboard Marine Corporation, Brunswick's leading competitor in the outboard motor business. Wayne Jones, vice president of strategic planning for OMC, told a Reuters reporter, "You have to agree what Brunswick did is a major move. It opens up more options that we have to consider, and certainly one of them is doing the same thing."

Attempting to play catchup, OMC purchased five small boat companies for about $120-million between December 1986 and February 1987. Analysts, even in the face of a potentially sour economy, saw the boat business booming.

"The ease of buying is greater now and the cost is less," said Elizabeth Bramwell, director of Gabelli & Company, a New York brokerage firm. "As long as money is available and as long as gas is available, the outlook is good."

It certainly looked that way in Skokie. Bayliner, which became the foundation of the company's U.S. Marine division, had added new 17- and 21-foot center console Trophy models to its offshore fishing line and new models to its Bayliner product offerings. At the start of 1988, it introduced a new line of pleasure boats called Maxum, consisting of upscale models that, it was hoped, would enable the division to expand into new markets through a separate dealer network. The Sea Ray division also added four new products in 1988, bringing to 50 the number of models it offered. At Mercury, sales and operating earnings continued to grow, bolstered by a 30 percent jump in international sales in 1987.

Zebco was enjoying great success during the 1980s, much of it due to the acquisition of the MotorGuide line of electric trolling motors and to the introduction of the Quantum line of fishing tackle to serve a broad-

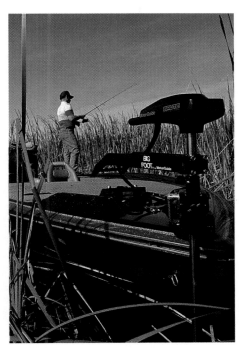

er segment of serious fishermen.

While Technetics continued to do well and the Brunswick Recreation Centers and Brunswick divisions displayed renewed vigor, results at the Defense and Industrial products divisions were about flat.

At the start of 1988, the company acquired four new boat manufacturers, with five brands; the Marine Group, Inc., MonArk Boat Company, Fisher Marine and Starcraft Power Boats. These brands were later brought together with the Spectrum boat operations, from the Bayliner group, to form the company's Fishing Boat division. The company would later add Wahoo! Boats to its offerings. And, in an effort to strengthen its high performance leadership,

The acquisition of MotorGuide trolling motors in 1984 broadened Zebco's leadership role in the fishing industry.

Zebco continued to extend its reach, when the introduction of the Quantum line in 1984 strengthened its appeal to more dedicated anglers.

This streaking flotilla
displays the brands
whose 1988 acquisition
led to the formation of
Brunswick's Fishing
Boats Division.

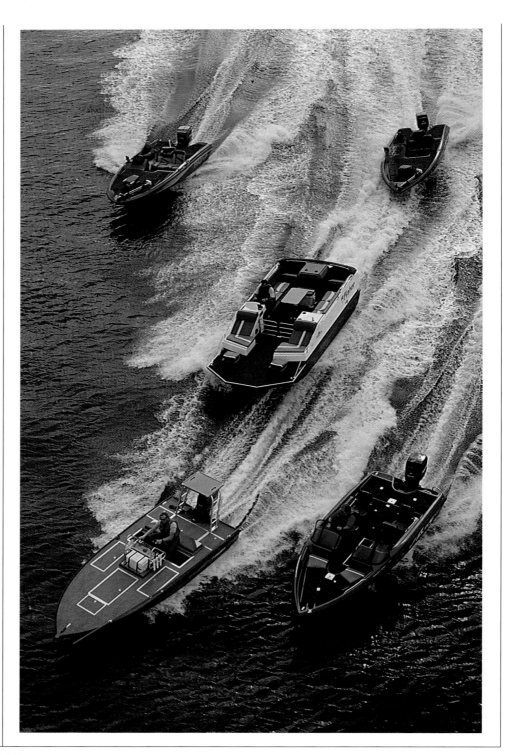

Mercury acquired Kiekhaefer Aeromarine. Perhaps as significant as that acquisition was the fact that it had been owned and operated by the only son of Mercury's founder, who would now become an executive of the company.

The face of the company had changed dramatically, nearly doubling the company's size, from $1.7 to $3.1 billion in revenues. Brunswick was once again recognized as a leisure and recreation company. For the second quarter, ending June 30, 1988, Brunswick had net earnings of $78.9 million on sales of $889-million; some $681.7-million of those sales coming from the company's marine businesses. No one seemed overly concerned about long-term sales or what might happen in an economic decline.

The picture looked pleasant and Florjancic proudly told a Chicago Tribune reporter in October, 1988, "We are clearly the General Motors of the boat business. We are the largest marine engine and boat company in the world."

Fisher *(above)* **and ProCraft are two of the seven popular brands which helped drive the growth of Brunswick Fishing Boats.**

16 *Sailing stormy seas*

The company emerges from near-crippling problems in the boating industry healthier and more firmly focused.

Asked to characterize business from late 1988 through 1991, Jack Reichert leaned forward and said, with chilling seriousness and simplicity, "Hell. It was hell."

Few would disagree. On the cold numerical surface, the figures were terrifying: boat sales fell almost 60 percent between 1988 and 1991.

"When we bought the boat companies and again after [the stock market crash known as] Black Monday I said to all of our marine people, 'I want you to do an analysis of what might happen if sales fell 10, 20 or even 30 percent,' from where we were in 1987. They did but had a hard time taking it seriously. 'It can't happen,' they said. 'It'll never happen. Business could never drop 30 percent. It hasn't happened in the history of the industry.'"

He paused to laugh.

"And, in a way, they were right. Business didn't drop 30 percent. It dropped more. If we had stopped at 30, the company never would have suffered to the extent it did. You can look at where we were and argue that if we were going to make mistakes in the boating business, at least we made them with the two best boat companies in the world. Now [early in 1995], as business is significantly better, I can smile a little bit more about the last few years. A little more."

The problems in the boating industry were primarily caused by two vicious blows: the recession that affected virtually all American businesses and a new 10 percent luxury tax on yachts that cost more than $100,000. Failure of boat manufacturers to react to rapidly declining retail sales exacerbated the problem as builders choked the pipeline through wholesale incentives.

The 65-foot *650 Cockpit Motor Yacht* exemplifies the expansion of Sea Ray's product offerings into larger-sized sport yachts.

Business had been very good at the start of 1988 and it was difficult to see storm clouds on the horizon. The company had great engine data but still was so new to the boat business that management was operating without a boat data base.

The difficulties began near the end of 1988. Sales of both boats and engines began to dip and most dealers had excess inventories. The result was felt at the plant level. As management struggled to fix matters, everything just got worse.

When those clouds arrived— understandably also shadowing the fishing industry—Reichert reacted swiftly, his quick response due in some part to his having shared the turmoil of decades' past when the bowling industry went bust.

"I had seen the bowling industry collapse," Reichert recalled. "I had learned, at a young age, you had to take decisive action. Even though I'm not a financial man, I learned that the thing you protect more than any other single thing is the balance sheet, so that the banks don't cut off your credit line. You must at all costs protect the underlying strength of your company. Survival is the goal. But survival is, in fact, a strategy."

In order for the company to survive, Reichert had to summon an inner strength, what he calls "the capacity to withstand a fair amount of pain and maintain my cool." Accurately assessing the severity of the free'fall of the marine business, the company acted almost a year in advance of competition with a $100-million write-off in order to right-size the marine business. Analysts quickly understood and voiced approval of the action, citing a precocious management style throughout the period.

That the marine industry would

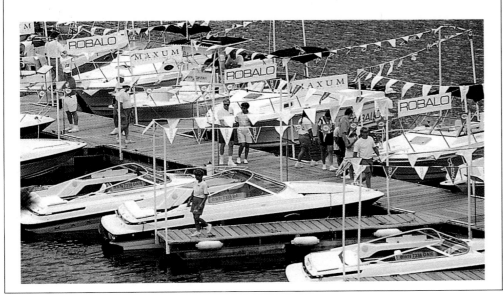

Even in the depths of the 1992 boating recession, US Marine dealers flocked to Georgia's Lake Lanier to witness the unveiling of the new Maxum and Robalo product lines.

rebound was not an issue. It had on four previous occasions in 20 years. And would again. But at what rate, and in what economic and environmental climate? "Hunker down and ride it out was not an option," Reichert told management at the marine units. "Brunswick must lead."

And lead it did. It was apparent that the exhilarating highs of 520,000 powered boat sales in 1988 would not return. Bottoming out at 260,000 units in 1990, the Brunswick Marine Group was formed to bring together all marine businesses to harness and leverage resources and right-size operations for the opportunities ahead. More focus was placed on quality and customers, manufacturing efficien-

cies and disciplined cost management. Everyone was committed to returning to previous levels of profitability consistent with shareholder expectations no matter what levels of sales volume. It was a strategy that would soon realize success.

"Jack's real strength was getting people to talk to each other," said John Charvat. Charvat, who as Zebco's president had devised the quality and customer based strategy which was the foundation of the division's growth in the 1980's, became head of the Marine Group and Executive Vice President of the company in 1989. "That's what really got us out of trouble. People would listen to Jack and say, 'Hey, this guy really does care. He doesn't speak values. He lives them'."

Astro, one of the Brunswick Fishing Boats which has exerted a strong appeal to the growing ranks of bass anglers.

An armada of Sea Ray boats, ranging in size all the way from 13 feet to 65 feet, are arrayed on the docks in front of the Division's Knoxville, Tennessee headquarters.

Brunswick would eventually close 14 boat plants and three engine plants. The company significantly reduced outboard costs by consolidating final assembly of all outboard motors from three plants to a single factory in Fond du Lac. The company provided retail rebates of more than $25-million to assist dealers in moving their field inventories; repurchased inventory from overstocked dealers; curtailed production dramatically to reduce inventories in the pipe line; and redesigned almost 50 percent of the boat product line to make the products more appealing.

Most painfully, the company was forced to eliminate some 8,000 jobs, or more than 40 percent of the company's marine employees.

"Too often in business one looks only at the financial numbers in a crisis," said Reichert. "But in any calamity such as this, those who suffer most are people. And many were unavoidably hurt by what had to be done."

For a view of what that was like, one only had to look to January 20, 1991, when Sea Ray's original plant closed in the small town of Oxford, Michigan. With it went a relatively tiny number of jobs—230 employees remained since layoffs had begun in 1987—but the community of 11,000 was stunned. It was a situation multiplied ten fold by all the boat builders across the country.

Company officials estimated that 100,000 boats had come out of the Oxford plant since it opened in 1962 and being known as the "Home of Sea Ray" was certainly more glamorous than had been Oxford's previous claim to fame: at the turn of the century it was known as "the sand and gravel capital of the world."

Marking the growth of Bayliner's successful cruiser line, this *2855 Ciera Sunbridge* debuted in 1993.

Zebco hailed the arrival of Brunswick's sesqui-centennial celebration with the introduction of this *150th Anniversary Limited Edition* Quantum baitcast reel.

Sea Ray's headquarters had shifted from Oxford to Knoxville, Tennessee, in 1978, but the 200,000-square-foot Oxford plant had continued to flourish, reaching top employment of 800 people in the late 1970s.

In reporting the plant closing, the Detroit Free Press quoted Oxford Township supervisor Rose Ann MacGuire: "It's definitely sad. [Sea Ray] has always been very good to the community and very supportive of the township."

While many of the plant's employees understood the economics of the decision, there were nevertheless voices filled with pain and resentment.

Not only were plants closing, but marine dealerships shut down, never to re-open. In fact, almost one-in-four dealers were forever gone.

"Decisive action had to be taken," said Reichert. "As difficult as it was for so many, we had to take control of a very bad environment."

To add to the difficulties, there were major changes in the senior management of the company due to retirements of division presidents at Mercury, Sea Ray, US Marine and Fishing Boat operations. When the smoke cleared, every direct report to the CEO except two of thirteen were in new positions. It was during this turbulent time that John Charvat and Dianne Yaconetti played key roles in the transition. Managers such as David Jones, Bill Barrington, Jim Hoag, Bob Steinway, Jeff Olson and Dan Horner became presidents during a very tough time in the marine industry. They were tested in the "heat of hell" and performed extremely well.

In recreation, Florjancic became president of the Brunswick Division and Jim Dawson replaced Charvat at Zebco. Both new presidents would be instrumental in significantly growing their businesses.

Brunswick's business, which had peaked in 1988, when the company earned $200-million on sales of $3.3-billion, bottomed out with sales of $2-billion in 1991. Things were better in 1992 as boat sales inched up and the company registered pre-tax earnings of $62-million.

In the process of change, everyone strived to become better listeners, hearing and responding to their widely divergent constituencies of dealers, boat builders, vendors and the recreational boaters and fisher-men. It was the new era of partner-ships that would differentiate Brunswick from other engine and boat manufacturers. It was a total commitment to customer satisfac-tion, the heart of the dealer support strategy.

Mercury Marine, Sea Ray, Bayliner/Maxum and the Fishing Boat companies began to forge strong alliances, earning respect through knowledge, combining

resources and working as one toward mutual success. It was Reichert's values in vivid reality.

While others pulled in their horns, the company signalled a will-ingness to invest capital to support a strategy that would lead the turn-around. As late as 1993, it was still tempting to close selected plants to bolster term returns. "It's around the corner," said Reichert, forecast-ing to industry publications and analysts that the rebound would be of significant magnitude. Not the five to eight percent seen by most. While others waited, Mercury Marine added capacity that in 1994 would be rewarded with unprece-dented gains in market share. For the first time ever, Mercury Marine challenged for the largest outboard share in the industry—in the world! And MerCruiser continued to grow share through technological and service leadership.

"It wasn't just the engine compa-ny, but all our brands enjoyed sig-

Swimming against the tide, Mercury Marine's bold decision to add capacity during the depths of the marine recession was rewarded with unprecedented gains in market share on the threshold of Brunswick's 150th Anniversary.

MerCruiser's established position as the the preem-inent stern drive engine brand continued to strengthen in the 1990's, due in no small measure to its technological and service leadership.

nificant gains in sales and earnings," Reichert proudly recounted. "Young managers who had known only the frustration of decline were now poised to harvest the rewards of consumer confidence in Brunswick.

Looking back over the period, former board member Pierre Rinfret sat with a reporter from *Fortune* magazine and offered this assessment: "What we've seen with the boat acquisitions and the general restructuring over the past five years has been a return by a company to its roots—back to the kind of business activities that have sustained it for nearly a century and a half. Reichert has reemphasized the historic evolution and foundation of the company and is building a new Brunswick on top of them."

In those five years, the company divested of those businesses that did not fit into the strategy: technical

The spectacular growth of bowling in Europe, the Pacific and Latin America fueled a dramatic expansion in Brunswick's bowling equipment sales during the 1980's and 1990's.

business such as Valve & Control, Technetics and Vapor were sold. Finally, the Technical Group (formerly Defense), which had during the early 1980s been the company's second largest division in terms of sales, was offered for sale.

"Many of these were good businesses," said Reichert. "It made a lot of sense to put them in the hands of people with a desire to grow those sorts of businesses. Selling them helped reduce our debt. The decision was especially difficult with regard to the defense business, since its roots went so deep into the company's history. But this strategy gave us the opportunity to better focus our energies on the leisure/recreation businesses."

Another strength during those difficult times were the consumable businesses of the company. Operations such as Zebco, BRC, Quicksilver parts and accessories and the consumer products sold by the Brunswick Division continued to grow as did bowling equipment.

A perfect day for fishing: A man, his boat, and his Zebco reel.

One of 1994's new product entries was the Quicksilver Sport RIB, the first of a new line of Mercury-powered rigid-hull inflatable boats.

Marking the progress of the Company's leadership of bowling's quest for Olympic recognition, International Olympic Committee, President Juan Antonio Samaranch rolls out the first ball at the 1992 opening of the Brunswick Bowling and billiard Recreation Center in the heart of Barcelona's Olympic Village.

Acquisitions, such as Martin Reel Company (fly reels) in 1991; the Browning line of rods and reels in 1991; and the Perry Austen and Pierce & Steven fishing operations in 1993 added further consumable sales. Also during that period, the company and Missouri-based Tracker Marine, largest aluminum boat manufacturer in the world, agreed to form a partnership, which was particularly vital in bonding

relationships with dealers who five years earlier had switched allegiance to other engine brands.

In April of 1993, the company completed its new world headquarters in Lake Forest, Illinois. There were encouraging signs on the domestic horizon that the marine business was coming back. Not far behind would be the increasingly important international segment.

As the company entered its

John Morris *(left)* **and Jack Reichert sign the documents which formed Brunswick's partnership with Tracker Marine.**

150th year in 1995, it could look back to 1994 with satisfaction. Sales and earnings were the third best in its history and the momentum was continuing into its anniversary year. The company was a leader in virtually every mar- ket it served and it was being led by a seasoned group of executives in all of its businesses.

It was an encouragingly gaudy way to enter the anniversary year. But numbers alone, except to Wall Street, do not a company make. The

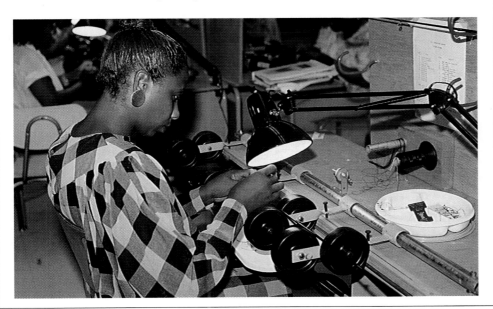

An innovative program begun by Zebco helped unemployed Americans learn skills that gave them a second chance for a future, and a job in this facility which Zebco opened in 1992. The plant brought jobs back to the U.S., by returning fishing rod production operations to their original domestic base.

success of a company, any company, rests with those who shape and share its goals, its vision. And the man who would lead Brunswick's 22,000 employees into the next years, the next century, was formally introduced in April, 1995.

Jack Reichert introduced the company's new President and Chief Executive Officer, Peter N. Larson, at the annual shareholders' meeting on April 26. Reichert, who would give up the title of Chairman in September, told the company's shareholders of the distinguised career that Larson had had with Kimberley-Clark and, most recently as Chairman of Johnson & Johnson's worldwide consumer and personal care group.

When his turn came to speak, Larson called Brunswick "the house that Jack Reichert built and to whom we owe a debt of gratitude for the foundation which he, the

Peter N. Larson

employees and the management have constructed... I salute Jack for all that he has done to elegantly cap 150 years of success."

April, 1993 marked the completion of Brunswick's new world headquarters.

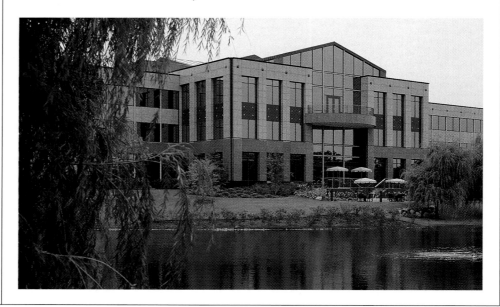

Epilogue

It would be a year of memories, celebrations and transition. The 150th year of the Brunswick Company would be marked by events and honors. The Illinois State Historical Society honored the company's longevity at a banquet. Special television features charted the company's long history. Chicago's Cultural Center was the site for a three-month long exhibit telling the company's story.

That story, filled with interesting characters, bold visions and the tumultuousness of doing business across a century and a half, has not been a difficult one to tell.

But it is a difficult one to end.

The company faces the future with the quiet, sturdy confidence possessed by only a handful of American companies, those select, rare few that have shown an ability to overcome the unpredictable and daunting challenges of a 150 year-long business adventure.

While other companies have vanished, Brunswick remains: its 150 years of knowledge and experience foretelling an even brighter future. The reasons for its success and continued vitality are complex, a combination of many elements — and thousands of people — that have formed this rich and unique portrait of American corporate life.

Art and Photography Credits